Knocking on Heaven's Door

Don Maclean

Watermead Publishing

"Knocking on Heaven's Door"

ISBN 978-1-907721-04-5

First Published 27th February 2014 by
Watermead Publishing Limited,
Watermead Centre,
St Joseph's, 12 Goodwood Road,
Leicester LE5 6SG
Telephone 0116 2207881

Edited by Fr John Daley IC

Presentation design and typesetting by Alison Kennedy
with acknowledgement to

Rory Maclean for his "Pestering Widow" cartoon

and a thank you to the ever-faithful Watermead editing team.

Watermead Publishing Apostolate
www.watermead-apostolate.com

Printed by AnchorPrint, Syston, Leicestershire
www.anchorprint.co.uk

Contents

Acknowledgements

Fr John Daley for his 'Saintly Factoids'

Gil Whale, editor of 'Catena', for inspiration

Page 82 **"If it's snowing ..."**.
*From the poem 'Forecast' by Stewart Henderson.
First published in his children's collection
'Who Left Grandad at the Chipshop?'
Published by Lion's Children's Books. Copyright 2000.
Used with the author's permission.*

*Every effort has been made to obtain copyright permissions.
If any reference has been omitted we apologise
and will correct in future editions.*

Other books by Don Maclean

MACLEAN UP SQUASH - Range Productions 1982

SMILING THROUGH (with Judith Wigley) - Lion Books 1996

FLYING HIGH - Hodder & Stoughton 2003

CLOSER TO HEAVEN - Hodder & Stoughton 2005

Introductions

A Personal Note

When I started presenting 'Good Morning Sunday' in 1990, the Producer, Michael Wakelin, asked me if there was anything special that I would like to include in the show. I said

"Well this is a religious programme; I feel that we should pray." For the next fifteen years I wrote topical prayers reflecting the events of the past week and the nation joined me in prayer at 7.55 every Sunday morning.

We regularly received letters from priests, ministers, Salvation Army officers, saying that they recorded the prayers every week and used them as a basis for prayer during their own services later in the day. I was delighted to be of help in that way.

When I left the programme in January 2006, several people suggested that I should write a book of prayers which could be used throughout the church year. I hope that this book will fill the bill and be a useful resource. The prayers are neither poetic nor biblical but they come from the heart.

Don Maclean

From Don's Friends

*"For many years 'Good Morning Sunday' was
a bright spot in the broadcasts of Radio 2.
Don Maclean presented religious news with an
enthusiasm that was infectious, involving listeners
in not only the features of the programme
but also in the prayers that he recited each Sunday.
I am delighted to see these prayers
gathered together in this publication.
The zeal and fervour that they express
will encourage many as they turn,
for at least a few moments each day,
to be in the presence of God and to be refreshed
in their relationship with God.
The title 'Knocking of Heaven's Door' is so apt.
The Lord invites us to be persistent in our prayer
and assures us that when we pray
he is certainly attentive to our cry."*

✠ Vincent Nichols
Archbishop of Westminster

*(As we go to print we have heard that Archbishop Nichols
will be consecrated Cardinal on 22nd February 2014)*

"Only Don Maclean, my friend and marvellous communicator, could come up with such a homely collection of thoughts and prayers!

There is nothing sanctimonious about 'Knocking on heaven's Door' but it is the kind of honest, real and humorous book that has the touch of the Almighty about it."

Rt Rev and Rt Hon The Lord Carey of Clifton,
former Archbishop of Canterbury

"In 'Knocking on Heaven's Door', Don Maclean offers a refreshing approach to a life of prayer that is enthusiastically shared from the insights and experience of his own faith. Whether it is a topical item for a particular day, or a reflection on the life of a saint, there is something for everyone to draw from. In a style that is both light and entertaining, Don's thoughtful reflections make the subject of prayer readily accessible to those who have a lot or little experience of prayer."

✠ Bernard Longley
Archbishop of Birmingham

From the Publishers

Watermead Publishing is part of the Watermead Apostolate – a sharing of faith through gifts, talents and time. We share music, cards, stationery and books, with everything produced being a chapter from someone's personal journey of faith. Through what we share we help and support various charities and good works.

The apostolate began in 1992 in a Catholic parish in Leicestershire, England, with the composing of hymns and a parish book of prayers. It was soon realised that everyone could be involved in such a mission of the Church, sharing their creative ideas, gifts, inspirations and generosity. "Watermead" was taken from the surrounding area so as not imply parochial or denominational ownership and this name has become the umbrella under which we offer our Christian message and ethos.

We believe everyone has valuable life experiences that, once given a voice, can reach out and connect with others, and Watermead is a sharing of those voices - offering people the opportunity to share their understandings of living their faith by whatever comes to them on their very individual paths towards God, enabling hearts to speak and communicate.

Watermead Apostolate

From the Editor

At Watermead we set a number of the Gospel parables to music. I wondered if we might record them - and knew we wanted a man of faith and with a sense of humour to sing them . . .

I thought of Don Maclean. I contacted his producer at the BBC who was amused at the suggestion and encouraged me to go ahead and ask Don directly. I did, and Don asked to see what we had composed.

He liked what he read and came to visit us to hear the music. So a project began which became 'Don Sings the Parables', and a friendship began with Don and Toni, Don's wife, which has extended to their coming with us on pilgrimage to Rome and Assisi, to Lourdes, organising retreats and sharing our faith ideals.

Don was so easy to work with. He told us of his work with the BBC, of his life in show business and of his Christian faith. He shared with us some of the prayers he had written for 'Good Morning Sunday' and said how much he would like, one day, to publish them.

'Knocking on Heaven's Door', is the book and we are privileged to publish it.

Fr John Daley IC

January – Saintly factoid:

21st January is the feast of St. Agnes, the twelve-year-old girl who died in Rome as a martyr sometime at the end of the third century. There are two churches dedicated to her memory – the one in the Piazza Navona, built over the prison where she was taken and put to death, and the other on the Via Nomentana where she was buried. At this second church on her feast day lambs are blessed in her honour and then given into the care of the nuns of St. Cecilia's in Trastevere (across the River Tiber). The wool that is later made from the fleece of these lambs is woven into scarves (palliums) and a pallium is sent to every new archbishop in the Church as a sign of his unity with the Pope in Rome. The night before being sent, the pallium is placed at the tomb of St. Peter, in a casket directly under the Papal altar in the basilica.

January: what a month. The start of the year, so much promise, so much to look forward to. Cast aside the old and bring on the new.

1st: The New Year is a time for resolutions and for new beginnings.

Help us to accept the power of your forgiveness, Lord, and realise that, with your love, it really is possible to start anew not just today but every day.

2nd: And as the New Year gets under way, let's pray for those people, young and old, who feel they have no purpose in life that they may be directed by the light of the Holy Spirit so that the New Year will herald new beginnings for them.

3rd: Today is the feast of 'the Most Holy Name'. We celebrate the name which is above all names, 'Jesus': a name to remind us constantly that God made man came down and dwelt amongst us, a name which means 'God is with us'. We rejoice that you call each of us by name and we pray that you will never leave our side.

4th: It's a day of prayer for retail workers. We pray for those working long hours in shops large and small, grand department stores or modest corner shops. We pray for their feet as shop workers rarely get the chance to sit down and we pray that they will find a smile in their hearts and on their lips for even the most difficult customer.

5th: This week is Arthritis Awareness Week. This condition which affects the joints, causing great discomfort and denying its sufferers mobility, is extremely common in our country.

We pray for those who bear their pain with dignity. Lord, make us sympathetic to their needs and ever ready to offer help and encouragement.

6th: On the **Feast of the Epiphany** Jesus Christ was revealed to the whole world. We think of the distance travelled and the hardships overcome by the Wise Men to reach Bethlehem.

We pray that we will have similar courage and perseverance to overcome any obstacle that prevents us from coming nearer to you. As they brought gifts, may we, too, offer to you the gold of faith, the incense of worship and the myrrh of compassion for others.

7th: Help us, Lord, to think before we speak that no words of ours will bring pain to another. Words can be used to comfort, to express love, to make people laugh. They can also be used to make people cry. Give sincerity to our words, especially those spoken in prayer.

8th: **The Baptism of the Lord**. At the moment of Baptism, I am as you intended me to be; totally at one with you, free from sin and united with all those whom you have called. May I renew that commitment every day of my life: to follow the way of the Gospel in the path of Jesus.

9th: Lord, give me hope; hope for myself, hope for my family, hope for my city, hope for my country, hope for my church and hope for the world. Show me where I can bring hope to others.

10th: We pray for all school children as they commence the new term this week. So often we hear the phrase 'If only I had my schooldays over again'. Lord, help our young people to make full use of their school years, ever striving to add to their knowledge and skills and to reach their full potential.

11th: Any small flurry of snow reminds me that each snowflake is unique, its pattern different from any snowflake before or since. We give you praise, Lord, for the tiny wonders of your universe.

12th: Help us to remember always to say thank you for the smallest act of kindness shown to us.

Happy are those who are humble; they will receive what God has promised. Grant me humility in all things, Lord.

13th: Heavenly Father, help us to pray, to use times of prayer whether spontaneous or planned to communicate our love, our hopes and our fears to you, our living Lord.

14th: It's about now that New Year resolutions come under pressure. Give me the determination, Lord, to always finish what I've started and, when I fail, to remember that you are there enabling me to start again.

15th: On dark January days we miss the sun but we know it's there, just hidden from view, waiting its chance to warm our lives. Lord, when fears form clouds and worries fill my mind, obscuring your presence, help me to remember your promise to be always with me.

16th: Regret is such a waste of time. Give us the strength, Lord, not to waste our thoughts on things we cannot change but to look to the future with energy and determination.

17th: This is the **Week of Prayer for Christian Unity**. We pray for the unity of your church here on earth. Although the different denominations may have different ways of worship and different theological emphases, we pray that all your children may learn to show love for one another and be united in honouring Jesus Christ as Lord and Saviour.

18th: Almighty God, creator and preserver of all, bless the people of this and every nation. We pray for all who are working to reconcile the divided, relieve the hungry and the oppressed, house the homeless and the refugee. May they bring your protection to the sorrowing, may they protect and care for the vulnerable. Govern the hearts and minds of those in authority and bring peace and hope to everyone. May your gift of peace flower as love and justice pervade our environment.

19th: It's Martin Luther King Day and our American cousins are having a day off.
We give thanks for his dream of peace between peoples of all races. We pray for those who still work today for peace and co-operation between people of different races and nations and faiths. Lord of peace, be with those who guide the destinies of the world.

Give them the courage to speak the truth and the humility to listen. We thank you, Father, for all those who have dreams and visions, give us the courage and faith to play our own part in bringing about your kingdom of love on earth.

20th: Today is the Feast of St Sebastian who was shot through with arrows because he refused to renounce his faith.

May the determination of Sebastian to remain true to his beliefs serve as an example to us all. We pray especially today for people all over the world who risk danger, persecution, even death for their Christian faith. Comfort and strengthen them, Lord, and shine your love into the hearts and minds of those who oppress them.

21st: St Agnes was a twelve-year-old girl martyred in Rome during the persecution of Christians by the Emperor, Diocletian, sometime at the end of the third century. There is a church in the Piazza Navona dedicated to her memory, apparently built over the prison where she was taken and executed by strangulation. There are plans to turn the dungeons into a museum. Today we remember St Agnes who is always depicted carrying a lamb.

It was you, Lord, who said to Peter "Feed my lambs". Father, feed my spirit that I may be brought closer to you and closer to the promise of eternity.

22nd: It's now more than a month since the shortest day. I don't know about you, but I feel a mix of pleasure and relief that it no longer gets dark at four o'clock. Today we remember those whose lives are perpetually darkened by depression or despair.

Hear us, Father, as we bring before you those who are discouraged and depressed. Bless with hope those who fear the way ahead; inspire with courage those who shrink from the challenges which they face; strengthen in us all the faith which recognizes your grace in the midst of failure and defeat. May your will for us all be achieved in your rule of justice and peace.

23rd: It's National Rhubarb Day. Who thinks up these days and could they possibly provide a reason for a prayer? It's said that you can pray about anything and, let's be honest, if it weren't for rhubarb, extras in TV dramas would have nothing to say.

As plants turn to face the sun and their leaves and branches reach out for the light, turn my face towards you, Lord, raise my hands in praise to you, the light of the world.

24th: Today is the Feast of St Francis de Sales, the patron saint of journalists. He wrote "religious devotion does not destroy, it perfects".

Help us, Lord, to heed those words of St Francis and strive for perfection through our devotion to you.

25th: Today is the feast of The Conversion of St Paul. Having dedicated himself to the persecution of Christ's followers, Paul's 'Road to Damascus experience' caused him to become the Church's first great missionary. He was beheaded for his faith but his writings live on to the present day, proving that the pen really is mightier than the sword.

26th: It's Australia Day, when Australians at home and abroad celebrate and publicly declare their pride at being Australian; these patriotic outpourings are neither discouraged nor ridiculed.

We give thanks, Lord, for the pioneering spirit of this nation and for the determination of its people. May nothing dampen the enthusiasm they have for their homeland.

27th: Holocaust Memorial Day. Genocide was not confined to World War II: throughout the twentieth century ethnic groups suffered persecution, torture and death at the hands of their fellow human beings.

We pray that this annual event will lead to tolerance and understanding between people of different backgrounds, that differences of race and creed will be celebrated, not feared, and that the barbaric acts of the twentieth century will not be repeated in the twenty-first. Keep our hearts clean of prejudice and hatred, Lord, and have mercy on us all.

28th: St Thomas Aquinas is commemorated today. Because he was quiet and shy, he was known to his fellow students as 'Thomas the Dumb Ox' but he went on to become one of the Church's greatest theologians.

May this serve as a warning to us, Lord, never to judge a person on first impressions but to dig deep and see the soul within.

29th: Lord enable me to stand tall before those who would seek to belittle me.

> "The Lord is my strength and my salvation,
>   whom shall I fear.
> The Lord is the stronghold of my life,
>   before whom shall I shrink."
> (Psalm 27)

30th: It's the anniversary of the assassination of Mahatma Gandhi. A moralist, teacher and reformer, he believed that social and political change could be achieved without bloodshed.

We ask that his philosophy of non-violence will be an influence for peace, not only in India but throughout the world, and we pray, Lord, for the repose of this 'Great Soul'.

31st: Today is World Leprosy Day. This dreadful disease which, in its later stages leaves victims horribly deformed, can now be cured. We reach out, in the name of Jesus who cleansed the ten lepers, to today's sufferers, stigmatised because of this ancient disease.   The Leprosy Mission's ambition is to eradicate leprosy completely.

Bless them, Lord, as they strive to achieve this goal.

AND ANOTHER THING . . . .

7th: *The Feast of St Raymond of Penyafort. He was a Dominican from Barcelona. Called to Rome in 1230, he brought together the many aspects of canon law establishing the documents used by canon lawyers for 700 years. It's said that he was nearly 100 when he died – remarkable for those times.*

12th: *The Feast of St Aelred, a 12th century English saint. Born in Hexham. He entered the monastery at Riveaulx, the first Cistercian house in England, and you can still visit the impressive ruins in Yorkshire. He later became abbot of Riveaulx during which time the number of monks reached 600. It has been said of him "no other English monk so lives in the memory".*

13th: *The feast of St Hilary who was a bloke, rather confusingly; all the Hilarys I know are women. He gives his somewhat feminine name to 'the Hilary term' of courts of law and universities which usually start on his feast day.*

Speaking of names; 13th January is also the Feast of St Kentigern – what a name that is! There is however hope for him because, in Scotland, he's St Mungo which has an all together better ring to it. Speaking of rings, the emblem of St Mungo is a ring and a fish; these refer to a legend in which St Mungo rescued an unfaithful wife from the wrath of her husband. Apparently she lost her wedding ring and it turned up in a fish – don't ask how, it's far too complex. The ring and fish are part of the coat of arms of Glasgow and Glasgow cathedral, despite having a statue of the protestant reformer, John Knox, outside, is dedicated to St Mungo.

25th: *Scots throughout the world celebrate Burns Night, keeping alive the memory of Scotland's foremost poet. His famous grace "...we hae meat and we can eat and sae the Lord be thankit" will have welcomed the haggis, reminding Scots to be ever grateful for their daily bread. May we always give thanks to the Lord for bounties he has laid before us.*

26th: *The Feast of St Timothy, the companion and helper of St Paul. Two of Paul's epistles are addressed to him. There's a famous statue called 'Timothy' in which he's seated and studying his own toes. I always think he should be the patron of people suffering from athletes' foot.*

31st: *Feast of St John Bosco, Founder of the Salesian Order. Apparently, as a young man, he was an acrobat, juggler and ventriloquist, but his true vocation lay in his great understanding of boys. He opened orphanages for homeless boys in Turin and also schools, he sought to make learning attractive and fun. Teachers of today could learn a lot from him.*

A THOUGHT
TO MAKE GOD SMILE

The best mathematical equation
of all time:
1 cross + 3 nails = 4 given

February – Saintly factoid:

14th February is known as St Valentine's Day – but not for some years has the Catholic Church celebrated the saint on this day. Thorough historical investigations during the 20th century discovered how little actual evidence there was for the stories of the lives of a number of the saints and Saints Philomena, Christopher and Valentine are three saints whose stories were declared to be legendary rather than factual. Saints Cyril and Methodius are now the saints remembered on the 14th February – they were two brothers who brought the Christian faith to the Slav peoples. Pope John Paul II made them patrons of Europe, representing the countries of Eastern Europe just as St Benedict represents the Western. Traditionally, 14th February is when birds in England choose their mates – the first day of spring: hence the old connection of St Valentine with declaring one's love.

Toni and I married in February, straight after pantomime, then went to Australia for our honeymoon. Lovely to get away from all that cold weather.

Don't you often feel glad that you live in a country that has seasons? Yes, it's great to sun yourself on a beach but would you want that heat constantly, all the year round? I'm all for a bit of ice to slip on, fog to get lost in and strong wind to blow the cobwebs away. February can supply you with all of that.

1st: It's World Widow's Day. St James [1:27] tells us to look after widows and orphans in their distress. We think of all those facing life without their soulmate. We think of the young women in our midst, widowed by recent conflicts, their hopes and dreams of lifelong unity have been shattered.
We ask your help, Lord, for those women bringing up children alone, give them the energy to meet the demands of single parenthood.

2nd: On this the Feast of the Presentation we recall the holy day on which Jesus Christ was presented in the temple, showing us that he was indeed the light of all nations.
We ask you, Lord, to fill the hearts of all believers worldwide with the light of faith.

16

3rd: It's the Feast of St Blaise. Most performers and public speakers know about St Blaise. Often you go into a dressing room and the array of linctus bottles, gargles and throat sprays make it look like a small branch of Boots the Chemist. Today we implore the intercession of St Blaise to ask the Lord's protection against throat infections, especially for the many people whose tonsils have joined the other side.

4th: It's Bowel Cancer Awareness Week. My Dad had an operation for cancer of the lower bowel, it resulted in a colostomy but it saved his life and I had him for another five years. I think of him often. "Those whom we love and lose are no longer where they were before; they are now with us wherever we go," said St John Chrysostom.

5th: It's the Feast of St Agatha - these are her words: "Inspire me, Lord, give me the will to act upon any words of encouragement, to trust in you and to follow my inspirations."

6th: Lord, often I feel that I am blind, deaf and lame in my faith. Open my eyes that I may see the needs of others, open my ears that I may hear your word, guide my steps that I will not falter in my quest to follow you.

7th: It's the anniversary of the first ordination of women in the Church of England in 1994.
We pray for every women priest who has fulfilled her vocation, often in the face of adversity, and ask that members of the Church of England will do all they can to avoid fragmentation and work as one body to bring men, women and children to know the love of your son, Our Lord Jesus Christ.

8th: On this day in 1587 Mary Queen of Scots was beheaded. Her motto was "In my end is my beginning". Lord, strengthen in me the belief that death is just a door to eternal life.

9th: We pray for a positive spirit in ourselves that we may live our lives with enthusiasm and a real joy in all the blessings you have given us. May your love shine from our faces this day and touch the hearts of those we meet.

10th: Every day you walk past me in the street, you are in each and every person I meet. Lord, help me to recognise you in others and to welcome the opportunity to be of service to you through them.

11th: It's the Feast of Our Lady of Lourdes, a day of prayer for the sick.

We ask your blessing, Lord, on the sick and the physically unable. Give them the strength to bear the burden of their cross and let them know that healing and wholeness awaits them in your presence. We pray for all people suffering from a life threatening disease that they may never give up hope. Help us to understand their suffering and, with your help, Lord, ease their pain.

12th: We know, Lord, that every person who has ever lived is unique. Help me to never envy another person or wish for any of their talents or characteristics. Let me realise, like Tigger, that the most wonderful thing about me is I'm the only one.

13th: A poor life this if, full of care, we have no time to stand and stare.

Give me a moment each day, Lord, to stand and stare at the wonder of your creation.

14th: Couples around the country are celebrating St Valentine's Day.

We thank you, Lord, for the capacity to love and be loved. St Paul tells us that love is patient and kind, not jealous, conceited or proud. Help us to realise that a loving relationship is something to nurture not to be taken for granted. We ask your blessings on those who have recently found love and on those who have been joined in love for many years. May the ones they love continue to bring joy to their hearts.

15th: Festivals such as St Valentine's Day often serve to highlight loneliness, so today we pray for the many single people in our churches and community who, through bereavement, divorce or other circumstance, live alone. We know that love comes in many ways: through family, through friends, but for those who are missing a special love. Lord, we ask that you draw close to them.

16th: You are the Lord my God who takes hold of my right hand and tells me not to fear. Never let me doubt, Lord, that when I stretch out my right hand you are there to help and comfort me.

17th: For every minute you are angry you lose sixty seconds of happiness.
Help me, Lord, to control my rage. Place your restraining hand on my shoulder before I boil over.

18th: On this day, in 1564, Michelangelo, the greatest artist and sculptor the world has yet produced, died.

We thank you, Lord, that we are still able to feast our eyes on the religious art of Michelangelo. The Sistine Chapel, the Pieta, many paintings and sculptures, all pay tribute to you, Lord, and to the talent you bestowed upon your servant. May all of us be ready and eager to use whatever talent you have given to us for the honour and glory of your name.

19th: Lord, you will light my candle and guide my way through the darkness. Father, sometimes the road ahead is dark and forbidding. I ask you to light my candle and guide my way through the darkness. Yes, Lord, guide me, teach me and strengthen me, until I become as you would have me be.

20th: It is National Nest Box Week, Lord, and we give thanks for all the birds of the air but particularly for the little birds. A robin, bluetit or thrush outside my window can bring a smile to my face that lasts all day.

21st: The winner of 'The Choir of the Year' will shortly be announced. We give thanks, Lord, for the skill and devotion of choir leaders who spend hours blending voices and co-ordinating movements so that individuals become one body praising and spreading your word through song.

22nd: It's World Scout Day. I was a scout in the days of pointed hats and naked knees and the endless search for a lost woggle. Uniforms have changed but the ethos of the Scout Movement remains the same. Lord, we applaud all organisations which give young people a purpose in life and a sense of adventure but also a moral aspect. May we, as the scout promise says, never fail to do our duty for God and Sovereign.

23rd: Polycarp! Sounds like a cross between a parrot and a goldfish but he was in fact one of the earliest martyrs. Today is the Feast of St Polycarp. Urged to forswear his religion and take an oath to the Emperor, Polycarp refused saying: "How can I blaspheme my King and Saviour?" He was then burned at the stake.
May we be like Polycarp, Lord, and may no blasphemous word ever pass our lips.

24th: Today is the Feast of the Chair of St Peter at Antioch. It's believed that St Peter spent seven years as Bishop of Antioch before setting off for Rome.

On this Festival we remember that St Peter was the first head of the Church on Earth.

We thank you, Lord, for the establishment and the propagation of the Christian Church and we earnestly pray for its preservation and its recognition in the furthest corners of the world.

25th: Weekday sermon: "God loves you. What are you going to do about it?"

26th: The opposite of faith is not doubt, it is self-opinion. Lord, I believe; help me to overcome my unbelief.

27th: Father Geoffrey, who taught Divinity at St Philip's Grammar School, would often say to us "Never be proud with God; there is nothing you can do that he will not be prepared to forgive".

Father, help me never to forget that, no matter how many times I get it wrong, you are always there to hear my words of apology and welcome me back into your arms. May I always forgive others in the same way.

28th: Lord, help us to rejoice in the variety and celebrate the richness of your creation. Show us your reflection in all people so that we'll know that they and we are your beloved children.

AND ANOTHER THING . . . .

2nd: *The Feast of the Presentation, which recalls the holy day on which Jesus Christ was presented in the temple as was the custom, under the Law of Moses, forty days after his birth. Mary and Joseph would have taken with them the purification offering of two turtle doves as demanded in the book of Levicticus and when they arrived they were met by Simeon whom God had promised would not die until he had seen the Messiah. Lots of babies who have been born during the last twelve months will be taken to church and blessed today. It's a lengthy blessing but the bit I like says:*

"May his Spirit comfort you and make you strong,
May he discipline you gently when you're wrong,
And in your heart may he give you a song;
This is my prayer for you."

4th: *Friday is the Feast of St Veronica. You'll remember her from the Stations of the Cross, wiping the face of Jesus with her veil. She is one of the four saints who surround the papal altar in St Peter's Basilica, Rome. I'm led to believe that the name 'Veronica' means 'true icon', because the true image of Christ was imprinted on the veil.*

24

10th:　　*The Feast of St Scholastica, the sister of St Benedict. After her brother went to Monte Cassino to establish his famous monastery, she founded a convent for her order of nuns. Benedict and Scholastica were buried in the same grave "so that death did not separate the bodies of these two whose minds had ever been united in the Lord".*

18th:　　*The Feast of St Colman - not the patron saint of mustard, despite the name, but one of the Celtic saints. He was a monk in the 7th century, first on Iona then Lindisfarne and finally Inishbofin – no I don't know where that is either but the name makes me want to go there. Having said that, I've been to both Iona and Lindisfarne and found both of them equally cold, bleak and damp. Still, praps that all adds to their charm.*

A THOUGHT
TO MAKE GOD SMILE

I was always told
to respect my elders - but
it keeps getting harder to find one.

March – Saintly factoid:

25th March is the feast of St Dismas, the good thief in St Luke's Gospel, who was promised paradise by Jesus as he was dying on the cross. Dismas is the patron saint of condemned criminals and protector against theft and thieves. On 15th March St Longinus is remembered. He is said to have been the soldier who pierced the dead body of Jesus with a lance. But the greatest remembrance in March is on the 25th, the Annunciation, the Angel Gabriel's carrying God's invitation to Mary to be the mother of the Messiah. Once the Church had settled 25th December as the day on which to celebrate Jesus' birth (a celebration first known of in Rome well into the 4th century) it was logical to step back the nine months and celebrate the wonderful Gospel moment of Mary and the Angel.

"Hail, full of grace, the Lord is with thee.
Blessed art thou amongst women,
and blessed is the fruit of thy womb, Jesus."

[Luke 1:28 & 42]

My birthday's in March. March comes in like a lion; I hope I did, I don't remember the occasion that clearly. It's a great month, lambs are being born, flowers are popping up, everything's bursting through.

1st: It's the Feast of St David, patron of Wales. We thank you, Lord, for the churches and chapels where the Christian faith has been fostered and maintained. We thank you for the Land of Song. May they continue to sing your praises and to keep a welcome in the hillsides and the valleys for all your faithful.

2nd: We applaud all those who will be supporting the Marie Curie Daffodil Appeal this week. We think today of those wonderful people: nurses, doctors, friends and relatives who have care of cancer sufferers.

We pray for all who are suffering with a terminal illness. Let them feel your presence, Lord, and be reassured that death is but a door between this life and the next. Stand with their relatives as they struggle to hold themselves together and to hide their anxieties from their loved one. Comfort them, Father, in their darkest hours.

3rd: It's National Book Week, Lord, and we thank you for those who have the gift of storytelling and who use that gift to transport us, their readers, to the far corners of the earth, to feed our hungry imaginations and to heighten our every emotion with the written word.

4th: The daisies are out! The word 'daisy' comes from the Old English 'Day's Eye'. The flower opens in the sunlight, faces the direction of the sun and closes as evening draws in. It clings very closely to the ground, reflecting the sunlight with a dazzling white brilliance, yet, as it begins to close, the tiny pink tips of the underside of its petals quietly come into view. It seems that the flower only exists to radiate the light that falls upon it, becoming ever more lovely as the rays strike its small, white petals.
Lord, there is nothing at all pretentious about a daisy. Most gardeners think of it as a weed but you called it a flower. It seems to me that, with your help, I could easily use the beauty, radiance and humility of the daisy as my role model in life.

5th: During this week we hold Women's World Day of Prayer when women unite before you, Lord.

We thank you for the strength and belief of women throughout the world and ask for your blessing on all those who draw close to you in prayer this day.

6th: On the feast of St Colette, the great reformer of the Poor Clares, Lord, I remember without you I am poor, I am destitute. As I make myself small, in my eyes, today help me to see how big you are.

7th: On Commonwealth Day we pray for all the diverse people of the fifty-three countries drawn together under the banner of the British Commonwealth of Nations. We thank you, Father, for the different cultures and beliefs which are represented in it and ask that you aid all member states as they strive to achieve its ideals of equality between different tribes, races and religious groups. May there be peace and shared understanding between us all.

8th: Today is the Feast of St John of God, the patron saint of nurses.
Bless, Lord, those who have care of the sick that by the comfort they give to others they may themselves be comforted

9th: Teach us, Lord, how to share our faith effectively, build community and, by prayerful lives of active loving concern for others, be your witnesses over all the earth.

10th: It is now medically possible to create a child in a test tube, decide whether that child should be male or female and genetically modify it for life. It seems that babies can be designed or customised. In 1987, the Vatican made it clear that they opposed test tube fertilisation and any scientific interference in human procreation.

We fervently pray that as doctors and scientists discover more about genetic medicine they will never lose sight of the fact that you alone are the Lord of all creation.

11th: My birthday: Jesus, master carpenter of Nazareth, wield well your tools in this your workshop so that I who come to you rough-hewn may be fashioned into an instrument for your use.

12th: On this day in 1945 a young Jewish girl named Anne Frank died in a concentration camp. She was just one of over a million Jewish children who died at the hands of the Nazi regime. The diary she wrote has become a monument, not only to her but to all those suffering children. One entry in the diary reads: "I want to go on living after my death

and therefore I am grateful to God for giving me this gift of expressing all that is in me."
We thank you that Anne has been immortalised by the diary she left behind.

13th: So often we read of terrible cruelty to children and even tiny babies in our own country. We pray for all who work to prevent such atrocity; the NSPCC and social workers who often come in for much criticism. We pray that criticism levelled at social workers will not result in their relaxing their vigilance and leaving youngsters defenceless.

14th: New English Bible published 1961, we pray for all those societies who print and distribute the scriptures. We give thanks for the generosity of richer nations who help poorer nations to spread your word amongst their people. May the Bible become available to all and may lack of resources never hinder that work.

15th: It's National Ideas Day, Lord. We thank you for the originality of thought that has brought forth some of the great inventions. We pray that all new ideas will be used for the benefit of mankind, not for its destruction.

16th: We pray today, not for the handicapped but for the emotionally disadvantaged who find it hard to accept someone who is physically disadvantaged. May all of us learn to love our neighbour as we love ourselves and to judge one another on who we are not what we can do. We pray for those who need special care and for those able to give it, that in accepting one another's strengths and weaknesses we can learn more of your love for us.

17th: On this the Feast of St Patrick, we give you thanks, Lord, for the Emerald Isle. We pray that the people of the four proud provinces of Ireland, Catholic and Protestant, already united under one saint, will unite to reject violence and rejoice in the continuing peace in the province of Ulster.

18th: It's Downs Syndrome Awareness Month. May we do all that we can to care for those with special needs and to support those who help them at work and at home.

19th: Today we celebrate St Joseph, an upright man, level-headed and prompt in action.
We ask your blessings, Lord, on all men bringing up and giving their love to children who are not their

own. May these children be ever mindful of the fact that anyone can be a father but it takes someone special to be 'your Dad'.

20th: On this day in 1852 'Uncle Tom's Cabin' was published. The author, Harriet Beecher-Stowe, said of it "I did not write it, God wrote it, I merely took his dictation."
Lord, I would welcome your dictation in my life. Give me the words, show me the plot so that when the story of my life is written, every reader will know that I followed your lead.

21st: The First Day of Spring reminds us of the circle of birth, life, death and rebirth. As we see trees in bud, flowers bursting forth and baby animals in the fields may they serve to remind us of the truth of the resurrection.

22nd: It's World Water Day. In some parts of the world, water is more precious than gold.
Lord, let us not take your gift of water for granted. Each time we turn on a tap, may we remember those who have to walk long distances and endure hardship each day to reach water.

23rd: It's the Day for the Elimination of Racial Discrimination.   Discrimination because of skin colour, language, nationality or culture is as pointless as deciding one flower has more value than another simply because a snowdrop cannot live in Africa or a mango doesn't grow in England.

Lord, remind us to take a good look at ourselves and our attitudes to others each and every day.

24th: Archbishop Oscar Romero was assassinated on this day. We pray for the repose of the soul of Archbishop Romero. He was murdered because he spoke out for the poor of El Salvador. Two weeks before he had said "I have been threatened with death. As a Christian I do not believe in death but in the resurrection. If they kill me I will rise again in the Salvadoran people. A bishop will die but the Church of God – the people – will never die." May his anniversary encourage us to do what we can to lift the curses of poverty and injustice from the developing world.

25th: On the Feast of the Annunciation, the Angel Gabriel told the Blessed Virgin Mary that she was to become the mother of Christ. We pray that we, too, may submit to your will in all things, Lord, and be ever willing to say: "Be it done unto me according to thy word."

26th: We pray for our farming community and for all others whose livelihood is rooted in the country. Lord, give them the courage to face difficult times and to look to the future with hope. We pray, too, for farm animals, asking you to ensure that we are ever aware of other creatures. Help us in future to be proper stewards of your creation and to treat animals with respect, putting their welfare before our gain. Lord, make all of us, both country and city dwellers, ever mindful of the delicate balance of nature.

27th: It's the Feast of St John the Egyptian, a hermit who lived a solitary life. We take the opportunity to remember all those people that live alone and pray that they may receive a visit from someone this week. Let us include all those people who have no-one to pray for them.

28th: Lord, sometimes we are so overcome by the suffering in your world that it's hard to pray. Help us to pray and to remember that you are the God of justice and peace. We remember those we know who are in despair and feel far away from you. May they know that in their suffering you suffer, too, and that you bring hope and light even in darkness.

29th: Today marks the birth of Winfield Scott Weeden who composed the wonderful hymn 'I Surrender All'. May we be alive to the sentiment of that hymn and willingly surrender ourselves to you in all things.

30th: A family is a mini church, a school of prayer, a haven of peace and a safe harbour from the world.

31st: This holiday weekend we pray for all those who travel, for those who will spend their weekend at work and for those who will have the opportunity to rest and relax. Bless, O Lord, the times when work is laid aside and grant that we may treasure our hours of rest and leisure as a time of refreshment so that we may serve you better.

AND ANOTHER THING . . . .

2nd: *The Feast of St Chad, the patron saint of the Archdiocese of Birmingham. The Roman Catholic Cathedral also bears his name. It was built by Pugin who was arguably Britain's finest ever church architect. And speaking of building, have you heard of Nicholas Owen? He was a builder of holes –*

priests' holes. During the reigns of Elizabeth I and James I, Roman Catholics hid priests in their homes, knowing that if they were found they would be executed along with those who had sheltered them. Owen built these tiny hiding places so skilfully that they were impossible to find. Sadly, he was captured and tortured to death; yet despite horrific treatment he refused to reveal the whereabouts of even one priest hole, knowing that doing so would mean the death of countless Catholics. In 1970, he was recognised as a martyr and canonised by the Church. In and around Birmingham there are many stately homes containing priest holes which can be visited. A real good idea if you fancy a day out this Summer.

6th *is the Day of Prayer for Temperance. Certain Christian denominations insist on temperance for their followers. I remember once going into a house which had a framed 'pledge' on the wall. At the age of 8 the lady in question had 'signed the pledge', vowing never to touch alcohol during her lifetime. Some commitment that! I'm sure that on a Monday morning most weeks there are innumerable young people who wish they'd been asked to make such a promise. Binge drinking is a major problem in our country these days.*

10th: The Feast of St John Ogilvie. Born in Scotland, he became a Jesuit priest and returned to his home land during the reign of James I. Saying mass was punishable by death; he was betrayed and sentenced to be disembowelled. Canonised during the last century there is now a great devotion to him north of the border.

19th: I'm a proud dad. I'm proud of my daughter, Rachel, and 19th March is her birthday. She's a happy girl and a wonderful mother to her two daughters. She's very involved with the Church and it's most gratifying for me to see that the Christian faith which has sustained me through my life is just as important in the life of my daughter – I must have done something right!

A THOUGHT TO MAKE GOD SMILE

If you look like
your passport picture
you could do with a holiday.

April – Saintly factoid:

23rd April is the day of St George, patron saint of England. His legend calls him a Christian knight whose journeying brought him to a city named Sylene. Near the city was a marshy swamp in which lived a dragon fed every day by the fearful citizens with sheep from their flocks. When the sheep had all been eaten one of the citizens came to be chosen each day by lot to be the dragon's meal. On the day of George's passing by it was the king's own daughter who was due to be served to the dragon. George rescued the princess, captured the dragon, brought it to the city and offered to kill it if the citizens agreed to become Christians. All agreed and were baptised. George is the patron saint of damsels in distress and of England. He was popular in England well before the Norman Conquest and was proclaimed Protector of England by Pope Benedict XIV in the 18th century.

In April, very close together, we celebrate the birthdays of three ladies who are important in my life: that's my daughter-in-law, Mel, on the 20th;

Her Majesty the Queen, whom I actually met when I received my MBE, on the 21st; and my granddaughter, Gracie, on the 22nd. Gracie and I love each other lots. I know that can't last, she's now a young woman, but I do hope that she'll always retain a soft spot for her Poppa.

1st: April Fools' Day: "Clowns and comedians are likely to have a high place in heaven because they must be near to the heart of God."(Thomas Merton)
Give me a sense of humour, Lord. Give me the grace to see a joke, to get some humour out of life, and pass it on to others.

2nd: Today is the anniversary of the death of Pope John Paul II who for over twenty-five years was the spiritual leader of all Roman Catholics and a beacon of hope for people of all faiths.
We give you thanks, Lord, for the life of the first Polish Pope. May the stoic acceptance of suffering he displayed during his final years be an inspiration to all who are sick and infirm. May your standard bearer, Blessed Michael, bring him into the holy light which you promised to Abraham and his descendants and may perpetual light shine upon him.

3rd: Today we remember the riots which took place in Brixton in 1981 and we pray that you will bring hope to those who feel that violence is the only way. Guide and strengthen those with the will and vision to affect a change. May they go boldly into their own communities, leading by example, to spread your word of peace, love and unity.

4th: We pray for all married people: for those newly wed, for those who have been married for several years and for those about to embark upon married life. May they never lose sight of the vows they made on their wedding day and may they be ever mindful of the sanctity of marriage.

5th: During this week we remember the genocide perpetrated in Rwanda. This slaughter which claimed innumerable lives was largely ignored by the rest of the world. We pray for the government of Rwanda, still trying to rebuild their country; we pray for the bereaved, many of whom lost every member of their family, and we pray for the murderers faced with the horror of their own actions.

6th: We think of all families who have been split apart by family strife and ask that they may swallow their pride and reconcile their differences.

7th: On World Health Day we pray that individuals will be prepared to take charge of their own well being and be ever mindful of the importance of fitness, diet and a healthy lifestyle.

8th: Today, the Birthday of the Buddha will be marked in many Eastern countries. We pray that we may strive to learn more about Our Saviour, Jesus Christ, about the gospels and epistles of the New Testament that in so doing we may be 'enlightened'.

9th: We mark the death of one of the great Christians of the 20th century, Pastor Dietrich Bonhoeffer. A German Lutheran minister, he saw the evil of the Nazi regime very early on. He did all he could to oppose Hitler and paid for this with his life just one month before the war ended. His final words were "This is the end – for me the beginning".
We ask your help, Lord, that we should, like him, be strong for justice, faithful to the truth and confident of eternal life.

10th: It's Cystic Fibrosis week. After years of painstaking research, doctors are now able to successfully screen for the gene which carries CF. We pray that this development will prevent the suffering caused by CF but there is still much to do. We ask you to call down the wisdom of the Holy Spirit on doctors and scientists involved in medical research that the quality of life of all those suffering from congenital defects may be improved.

11th: Today is the anniversary of the liberation of Buchenwald, the first of the death camps to be reached by Allied soldiers. Those who survived the concentration camps will never fully recover from the barbaric treatment they received.

We ask you, Lord, to be near them. We pray that you will sooth their minds as memories of loved ones who died come flooding back. Help us all to show compassion to anyone whose life is marred by tragedy.

12th: The day on which Uri Gagarin became the first man in Space. Do you envy him? I do. So few people have viewed this Earth in its entirety.

We thank you, Lord, for the spirit of adventure which prompts brave men and women to risk life and limb to push back the frontiers, allowing the human race to appreciate even more of your creation.

13th: We thank you, Father, for the gift of prayer by which we are able to communicate directly with you, the Lord of all creation.

14th: I have several times visited the fortress of Massada overlooking the Dead Sea where, in 73AD, 967 Jewish zealots chose death rather than capture by the Roman army. Modern day Israelis take great inspiration from this 'heroic' act.

Lord God, we pray that those living in the Middle East today will never be in a position where death is preferable to life in you.

15th: At 2:27 am on 15th April 1912, the Titanic slipped beneath the icy surface of the North Atlantic. This tragedy is still spoken of in hushed terms a century later. There are more liners and cruise ships than ever before sailing the high seas.

We ask that we will never underestimate the power of the ocean. We pray for all who sail, for pleasure or profit; bring them safely to port, Lord.

16th: It's the Feast of St Bernadette. We give thanks, Lord, for this saint of your church whose faith has inspired so many Christians and given so much hope and encouragement to the sick and the handicapped. We give thanks, too, for the Blessed Virgin Mary, Our Lady of Lourdes, through whose intercession many are able to place their prayers and petitions before her beloved Son.

17th: Zimbabwean Independence. We pray for all the people of that troubled country; farmers who fear that their lands will be confiscated, people living in poverty facing an economy in collapse, those who want change but who are fearful of despotism. Lord, pour out your spirit on your people – where there is despair give hope, where there is hatred sow love, where there is fear grant your peace.

18th: It's the anniversary of the San Francisco Earthquake which took place in 1906. Every year earthquakes occur in the world. We cannot imagine the terror of being buried alive, of survivors too afraid to go back into any building.
We think of those left homeless through natural disaster and we pray, Father, that, through your love, shattered communities may be healed and broken lives rebuilt.

19th: We pray for all elected Members of Parliament that they will open themselves up to guidance from you, Father, and that, like Solomon, they will serve their constituents with wisdom and justice.

20th: It is Parkinson's Awareness Week. We pray for all who suffer from Parkinsonism, those whose daily life is a struggle against stiffness, rigidity and tremor. Their hopes of a cure are constantly being raised then dashed. We pray, Lord, for a breakthrough in research that will ethically improve the quality of life for all sufferers.

21st: Birthday of Her Majesty the Queen. Lord, we thank you for our sovereign lady, Queen Elizabeth, who has reigned over us for more than sixty years.
We thank you for her example of duty and obedience, courage and fidelity. We pray for her continued strength and energy and ask you to help this nation, made up of people from many ethic backgrounds and many different faiths, to combine to ensure a joyful day for the lady who is Queen to us all.

22nd: On United Nations Earth Day, we give you thanks, Lord, for the beauty of this planet on which you have placed the human race. It is a humbling thought that, for all its vastness, the Earth is but a speck in your universe.

23rd: It's St George's day. He has been the patron of England since 1350, the year in which Edward III instituted the Order of the Garter in George's name.

Most of his deeds are known only to God but we do know that he was a Christian knight, true to the ideals of chivalry: bravery, honour, courtesy, fidelity. In this day and age there are still dragons to be slain.

Help us, Lord, to care for England, its countryside, its people and its reputation around the world. Help us to celebrate all that is good in merry England.

24th: It's the World Day for laboratory animals. We ask, Father, that this day will serve to focus our minds on the delicate balance of nature and on the serious responsibility you have given us in making us custodians of this planet and all the creatures in it.

25th: Anzac Day. Every year, hundreds of young people from Australia and New Zealand travel to Gallipoli at this time. They sleep overnight in Lone Pine Cemetery where so many of their countrymen lie. In the morning they participate in the Memorial Service. These are the words spoken by Kamul Ataturk at the first memorial service: "You, the mothers who sent your sons from far-away countries, wipe away your tears. Your sons are now lying in our bosom and are in peace. Having lost their lives on this land they have become our sons as well." Lord Jesus Christ, Prince of peace, remember the fallen.

26th: It's International Turn-off TV week. We're told that adults in Great Britain watch 3½ hours of television per day with children often watching more. Help us, Lord, to see this week is a chance for parents and children to be active and to do things together, a chance for all of us to be doers not watchers. We pray, too, for TV programme makers that they will be ever aware of their responsibility in shaping young minds.

27th: South Africa National Day – Freedom Day: After years of discrimination it is now possible for South Africans, no matter what the colour of their skin, to vote on their country's future. We thank you, Lord, for the vision of Mandela, Le Klerk and Tutu and we echo the prayer of Archbishop Worlock: "God bless Africa, guard her children, guide her leaders and give her peace."

28th: In the year 1770, Captain Cook landed at Botany Bay. Australia, once a land of penal servitude, has become a land of opportunity. Many of us have relatives who have made a new life on the other side of the world. While they enjoy your bounty of sea and sun, may they remember to keep in touch with loved ones left behind and may the traditional links between our two countries strengthen and grow.

29th: St Catherine of Siena, patron saint of Italy, was said to be the most influential woman in the Church during her lifetime. Her body is in the Church of Santa Maria Sopra Minerva which is very near to the Pantheon in Rome. Christ spoke to her to say "The only way you can serve me, Catherine, is in service of your neighbour."

May we, like Catherine, never forget your commandment to love our neighbours as ourselves.

30th: It's the anniversary of the swearing in of the first President of the United States of America. Over two hundred years later this has become the most important political office in the world.

We pray that the present and future presidents will use their power and influence to lead the Western world with wisdom, courage and humility and that, like George Washington, they will be ever mindful that there is a higher authority to which we must all pay deference.

AND ANOTHER THING . . . .

4th: The Aldermaston Marches were a feature of the 50s and 60s. The first one took place on this day in 1958. We give thanks that nuclear power has, in the main, been used for peaceful means and trust that it will continue to be so.

During April we mark Save the Children Week, which highlights the plight of children who have been robbed of their childhood. One tragic area is that of child soldiers, stolen from their homes and forced to fight by guerrilla groups. We beg your help, Lord, for 'Save the Children' as they attempt the difficult task of reuniting these lost children with their families.

A THOUGHT
TO MAKE GOD SMILE

A prayer
for my desk -
"God bless this mess".

May – Saintly factoid:

19th May used to be the Feast day of Pope Celestine V but he has quietly disappeared. His is a sad story. He was Peter the hermit at the end of the 13th century in a time of rivalry and jealousy amongst the cardinals of the Church over the election of a new pope. For more than two years the nine cardinals were unable to agree on a successor to Pope Nicholas IV who had died in 1292. Peter rebuked the cardinals for failing God and the Church and they retaliated by electing him as a compromise candidate! The task was beyond him and after six months he begged to be allowed to resign. He knew what a failure he had been and what harm his poor administration was doing to the Church. A holy man will not make a good pope unless he has the qualities required for such an important position. The Church recognised Peter's (Celestine's) sanctity but agreed with his standing down from the papacy.

It's May, it's May, the lusty month of May.
The lusty month when everyone
throws self control away.

('CAMELOT' Alan Jay Lerner)

1st: It's the feast of St Joseph the Worker and so we ask your blessing, Lord, on human work. Bless particularly those who work with their hands, as St Joseph did, give them pride in the finished product, the tribute to their skill. We also ask that you will care for those who work in dangerous occupations, underground, at altitude, on the high seas: grant them your protection, Lord.

2nd: The Feast of St Athanasius, Bishop of Alexandria, a man described as being small in physical stature but of towering spirit.
We give you thanks, Lord, for all people striving to make up for some perceived deficiency; fill them with your spirit.

3rd: Today is World Press Freedom Day. Lord God, who chose the written word to speak an eternal gospel to every age, give to those who handle words as journalists a constant loyalty to truth and a heart concerned with wisdom. May they raise, not lower our moral standards and increase, not diminish, the true welfare of mankind.

4th: On this day in 1954 a mile was run in under four minutes for the first time.

Lord, we rejoice in the desire you have placed in athletes to run faster, jump higher and throw further. Each of us has our own personal race to run. May we run that race to the best of our ability and always for your glory.

5th: It's the anniversary of the formation of The Religious Tract Society which today publishes Religious literature in 270 different languages.
We give thanks, Lord, that your word is accessible to so many. Surely one of your greatest gifts to us is the ability to read: open a book and there is a direct entry to worlds within the minds of others.

6th: Anniversary of the opening of the Channel Tunnel. That strip of water that has saved us from invasion for nearly one thousand years was finally conquered in 1994 by a great feat of engineering. May we dispel the negative and look for the positive benefits: ease of travel, ease of trade and a better relationship with Europe of which we are part.

7th: National Cot Death Appeal Week. Despite recent breakthroughs cot deaths are still the largest cause of infant mortality in the first year of life. We pray for those who have lost children in this way. Comfort them as they mourn, let them find hope and peace in you, Lord, and may the efforts of researchers and fundraisers result in the eventual prevention of these tragic deaths.

8th: It's VE Day. Victory in Europe was bought at a price: millions paid with their lives, their limbs and their minds.
We ask you, Lord, never to let us forget the debt we owe to those who made the ultimate sacrifice and we pray that, as with every remembrance of war, our determination to maintain peace will grow.

9th: Europe Day: The countries of our continent, so eager to make war on one another during past centuries, are now joined together by treaties and trade.   May we retain and celebrate our cultural differences whilst maintaining a strong desire for peace.

10th: We pray for all who seek public office that they will resist the temptation to abuse their privilege and position, that they will be men and women of integrity and seekers after truth, ever mindful that the moral bankruptcy of one of their number brings the whole of politics into disrepute. We pray, too, for our judicial system that it will continue to show that no-one is above the law.

11th: Grandparents are always keen to tell one another about their grandchildren and those of us who have grandchildren ask you, our Heavenly Father, to pour down your blessings on those small people who are so dear to us. May our example lead them to a life-long relationship with you so that they may keep the faith of our fathers living still.

12th: On International Nurses' Day we remember with gratitude Florence Nightingale and the small band of selfless women who founded this noble profession. We pray for nurses throughout the world, ministering to the sick and to the terminally ill, that they will always be true to their calling.

13th: Feast of Our Lady of Fatima. In 1917, The Blessed Virgin Mary appeared to three children in Portugal. She taught them this prayer:
"O my Jesus, forgive us our sins, save us from the fires of hell, lead all souls to heaven especially those in most need of your mercy."

14th: Feast of St Pachomius, the first monk to bring hermits together to show that living out one's faith in community was preferable to doing so in solitude.

We pray for a positive spirit in ourselves that we may live our lives with enthusiasm and a real joy in all the blessings you have given us. May your love shine from our faces this day and touch the hearts of those around us.

15th: It's the United Nation's International Day for Families. The family is said to be under threat but the family unit still remains the best environment in which to nurture children.

We remember today all those families who, for one reason or another, are parted, that your love will keep them forever in one another's hearts until they can be together again. We pray for the family of the Church in which we are all brothers and sisters in Jesus Christ. Help us to settle our differences and work together as the family we should be.

16th: We ask you, Lord, to keep us ever mindful of the pressures and responsibilities upon our pastors and our religious leaders. We thank you for these men and women who have followed their calling and pray that you will give them patience, determination and vision to fulfil your will in their ministry.

17th: United Nations' World International Telecommunications Day. Recent years have seen an explosion in telecommunications: mobile phones, satellite navigation, the world-wide-web, all inventions intended to be used for the good of mankind. Facebook and Twitter were only developed to help people to keep in touch with one another. Now there are those nicknamed 'trolls' who use such sites to insult and denigrate others. It would appear that the legacy of telecommunication will be that it enabled the human race to sink even lower than ever before. We can only pray that those who see the internet as a means for evil ends will grow up before they do any lasting damage.

18th: Teach me to be generous,
teach me to serve you as you deserve,
to give and not to count the cost,
to fight and not to heed the wounds,
to toil and not to seek for rest,
to labour and not to seek reward,
except that of knowing that I do your will.

Prayer for Generosity *(St Ignatius of Loyola)*

19th: This day in 1971 saw the first performance of the musical 'Godspell' based on the Gospel according to St Matthew. Grant that we, Lord, may live by the words of its most well-known song and

"See you more dearly, love you more clearly and follow you more nearly day by day."

20th: In National Epilepsy Week, we pray for all those who live an uncertain life because of this condition. We pray for all doctors and scientists working to ease the plight of the 300,000 people in this country who suffer from this disorder. Help us, Lord, to take the opportunity this week to learn more about epilepsy and use that knowledge for the benefit of others. We ask you to keep us ever mindful of the pressures and responsibilities upon our pastors and our religious leaders. We thank you for these men and women who have followed their calling and pray that you will give them patience, determination and vision to fulfil your will in their ministry.

21st: On this day in 1927 Charles Lindbergh landed in Paris, the first man to fly the Atlantic. With only a single engine and minimal navigation aids that takes faith.
Give me faith, Lord, to always put my trust in you.

22nd: St Rita, patron of infertile couples, and we pray for all those couples who, despite all efforts, have not been blessed with children. Those of us who have children cannot fully appreciate the anguish of their situation. Help them, Lord, to realise that they have not been rejected as parents. Bless them to find purpose in life that will be both rewarding and fulfilling.

23rd: No matter in which church we worship, praising you and doing your work is what truly matters. Help us always to make that our first priority.

24th: The day in 1738 when John Wesley became convinced that all people in Britain must, at all cost, hear 'The Good News of Salvation'. Wesley is said to have travelled 26,000 miles and to have preached 40,000 sermons.

Lord, we thank you for the example of John Wesley. May we never miss the opportunity to spread your gospel. We pray for all Methodist Churches. May those who preach in them, both ordained and lay people, be filled with the fire and enthusiasm of Wesley whenever and wherever they speak.

25th: Missing Children's Day. We cannot imagine the anguish of parents who have no idea where their child is.

We pray that these youngsters will swallow their pride and realise that one short phone call will set the mind of a mother or father to rest. May they realise that no matter what they have done, they will, like the prodigal son, be welcomed with open arms.

26th: I was educated at St Philip's Grammar School in Birmingham. Our school patron was St Philip Neri whose feast it is today. St Philip, the saint of gentleness and kindness, a man of humour and laughter with a great devotion to the Holy Spirit. "Holy spirit, soul of my soul, enlighten, guide, strengthen and console me."

27th: Feast of St Augustine of Canterbury. There are many words attributed to him but these are my favourite: "Do not be afraid to throw yourself on the Lord. He will not draw back and let you fall. Put your worries aside and throw yourself on him. He will welcome you and heal you."

28th: Today is the anniversary of the founding of Amnesty International.
We pray for their concern for prisoners of conscience throughout the world. Protect and encourage them in their work. We pray for those who have no rights, those who are enslaved or imprisoned because of their religious and political beliefs and victims of torture. Help end their despair, Lord. We thank you

that in your sight all people are equal and of infinite value. Help all of us to work for your justice on earth.

29th: On this day in 1953 Hillary and Tensing achieved the first ever conquest of Everest.
Lord, foster in us all the desire to reach the heights that we may come closer to heaven and closer to you.

30th: The Feast of Joan of Arc, the Glorious Maid of Orleans, whose unflinching heroism, constancy and devotion brought her victory in battle and a place in heaven. We celebrate the short life of this heroic saint whose deep faith and patriotism ensure that she will be forever remembered. "My voices were from God" she declared as the flames consumed her in the Market Place of Rouen.
May all your servants, Lord, be ready and eager to hear your words and to act on them.

31st: The Feast of the Visitation of Mary to her cousin, Elizabeth. I've been to Ein Karem, just a short journey from Jerusalem. A church now stands on the site of the house of Elizabeth and Zechariah. As Our Blessed Lady carried Jesus within her on that long journey, then brought him into the world, may we carry Christ with us every moment of our lives.

AND ANOTHER THING . . . .

2nd: *Feast of St Athanasius. He is one of the eight great doctors of the Church together with Ambrose, Jerome, Augustine, Gregory, John Chrysostom, Basil and Gregory of Nazianzus.*

4th: *The Feast of the English Martyrs. (It's May 4th, 'Star Wars Day', so may the fourth be with you!) During the reigns of Elizabeth I and James I, it was a capital offence to say mass in England. Many young men went to the continent to study for the priesthood with the sole intention of returning home to bring the mass and sacraments to the persecuted faithful. Many of them, together with the lay people who assisted or sheltered them, were put to death. As these 324 men and women were martyred for their faith, we believe they are now enjoying their eternal reward in heaven.*

6th: *Anniversary of the opening of the Channel Tunnel. Napoleon wanted to build a tunnel under the Channel so he could invade England. I'm surprised he didn't try to part the waters as Moses did. The Channel is no longer a barrier: that's progress, but something deep inside me keeps saying it should be filled in.*

19th: *Feast of a great English saint – St Dunstan. So many think that Dunstan is patron saint of blind people but in fact he's the patron of metal workers. He's also credited with being the person who created the Coronation Service in 973, still used today – they made things to last in those days!*

A THOUGHT
TO MAKE GOD SMILE

If you want a rainbow
you have to
put up with the rain

June – Saintly factoid:

St Ferdinand of Lisbon was born in 1195 and died in 1231. He is one of the most popular and famous saints in the history of the Church. We know him as St Anthony of Padua: Anthony was the religious name that Ferdinand chose when he became a Franciscan friar and by which he was always known; and Padua is the city where he died – known and loved throughout Europe. He is the patron saint of people who are looking for lost articles: "Dear St. Anthony, there's a good man; find mother's glasses as quick as you can" is an old Liverpool rhyme. St Anthony is remembered on 13th June.

June is busting out all over. She should never have had that second helping of pudding.

1st: Driving tests were first carried out in Great Britain on this day in 1935. In 1970 Miriam Hargrave passed her test at the 40th attempt – how's that for determination!

We ask you, Lord, to watch over all of us who sit behind a steering wheel. Make us realise that we should do nothing to endanger life, ours or others.

2nd: On this the Feast of St Elmo, the patron saint of sailors, we pray for all who travel on the oceans of the world. Through stormy seas and calm, through long voyages and loneliness, may your surrounding love and presence be always with them, Lord, protecting them from peril on the sea.

3rd: The stress of modern living is everywhere in evidence. It's said that a third of all medical problems in our country are concerned with mental health.

We pray for all those who are mentally damaged, those who find the world frightening and too much to cope with, that they may be reassured of your eternal love. We need to review our attitude towards the mentally unable. Replace our ignorance with understanding, our fear with compassion. Show us that by making a real effort to come into contact with both the mentally and physically handicapped, they will learn from us and we shall learn from them.

4th: Laughing is good exercise, it's like jogging for the insides. It's National Smile Month.
Help us to smile today, Lord, and with our smile to bring joy into the lives of those we meet.

5th: World Environment Day, Lord, and we ask you to guide us in our efforts to be good custodians of the planet that you have entrusted to our care. Everything, even the air that we breathe, comes from you. May we value all living things. Forgive us, Lord, for all that we take for granted, all that we abuse, all that we ignore or fail to see around us. Curb our destructive ways and lead us to realise that the resources of this planet are for the benefit of all people, not just of the few.

6th: It's D-Day. In services both here and in France, the British, Canadian and American servicemen who died as a result of that event will be remembered by relatives and comrades. Many soldiers who survived the battle will revisit the Normandy beaches, their thoughts filled with the faces of friends destined never to grow old as they have grown old. We pray for the repose of all those who died. A fitting memorial to them would be lasting peace.

7th: We ask your blessings on all those men and women presently preparing to be ordained that they may be radiant witnesses of your merciful love.

8th: Today is the Day of Prayer for Human Rights. We pray for the exiled, the tortured and the oppressed. There are too many countries in the world which have an appalling Human Rights record. We pray that pressure will be brought to bear on these governments so that abuse of human rights will become a thing of the past.

9th: The Feast of St Columba. My milkman's named Columba. When he comes for his money I must remember to give him a yoghurt to mark his feast day. Columba is described as "loving to everyone, happy-faced, rejoicing in his innermost heart with the joy of the Holy Spirit".
Dear Lord, may we be like St Columba!

10th: During National Diabetes week we pray for the many people in this country who stoically endure the inconvenience of this condition. We give you thanks that it is possible to lead full and rewarding lives even when our bodies sometimes let us down.

11th: It's the feast of St Barnabas, described as a man full of the Holy Ghost and of faith.

I thank you, Lord, for the gift of faith – faith to know that I can trust you to uphold me when I feel fear trying to overwhelm me. Give me faith that is uncluttered and simply enables me to believe in you and in all that you do.

12th: On this day in 1667, the first blood transfusion was performed. Nowadays, this is a regular occurrence but the blood has to come from somewhere.

So we give thanks, Lord, for blood donors, those men and women who give of themselves and in so doing ensure the survival of accident victims, new mothers and those undergoing surgery. May they know that their social conscience is truly appreciated.

13th: St Anthony of Padua was always important to me when I was a lad. If you mislaid something, you prayed for the intercession of St Anthony and invariably it would turn up.

Father, let us always be grateful for possessions and people that are returned to us. Like the shepherd with the lost sheep, the widow with her lost coin or the father of the Prodigal Son, may we remember to rejoice and give thanks for our good fortune.

14th: We pray for all those for whom alcohol has become a problem, for the addicted and those who live with them. We pray, Lord, for alcoholics: help them to find the strength to say no and a vision of what life would be like without drink. We pray, too, that they may be surrounded by the love and support of families and not be deserted in their time of need.

15th: On this the Feast of St Vitus we thank you, Lord, for your gift of dance; for its ability to move us, to express feelings we sometimes find hard to put into words. We give thanks, too, for the special power of dance with its universal language to speak to people across the world and time. Help us appreciate its beauty and variety and to use it for your glory.

16th: South Africans are celebrating Soweto Day. The riots in that township certainly had a bearing on the overthrowing of 'Apartheid'.
We pray for the post-apartheid government that they will continue to protect the weak and promote a society where freedom, justice and opportunity are given to all and where your name is honoured.

17th: Lord, there's only one of me; I have only two hands, one brain and twenty-four hours each day. Help me to use all that you have given me to the full.

18th: At this time of year pilgrims from all over Europe set out to walk to the Shrine of St James at Santiago de Compostela in Spain. It is a long and arduous journey needing courage and determination. Lord Jesus, yourself the way, the truth and the life, grant to those who tread the steep and stony path to Compostela a sense of awe, wonder and holiness. Be there in each step they take and bring them home in peace.

19th: During National Hospice Week collectors have been out in the streets selling yellow sunflower badges.
We thank you, Lord, for the wonderful work of the hospice movement. We ask your blessings on all who are suffering with terminal illness, on their families and on all who care for them.

20th: On World Refugee Day we pray that we will have compassion for all refugees, especially those in fear for their lives. Lord, may the countries that welcome them see them not as a burden but as their brothers and sisters in great need.

21st: In 1633, the astronomer and philosopher Galileo was put on trial for making statements about our solar system which we now accept are true.

It wasn't until 1992 that the sentence passed on him by the Inquisition was formally retracted by Pope John Paul II.

Lord, we pray for the hierarchy of your church which has a duty to stand against heresy, but let it be enlightened and open to new thoughts and ideas, bearing in mind that all scientific discovery must surely come from you.

22nd: The Wimbledon Championships are upon us; each year they bring so much pleasure to those who enjoy sport.

We thank you, Lord, for the dedication and skill of the outstanding sportsmen and women who participate. May they set for themselves the highest standards of personal and professional behaviour, both on the court and off, so that those who follow them may learn from their example of fair play.

23rd: Lord, we thank you that you have blessed some people with wonderful voices but we know that whether our voices are like nightingales or crows we can lift them in praise to you. We thank you for the privilege of worship and communion when we sing praises to you. We know that you accept our praises as a Father accepts a gift from a child and it encourages us to give thanks to you all the more.

24th: This is the time of year when often we read of forest fires. The fact that many fires are started deliberately only adds to the anguish. It's a time when firefighters, rightly dubbed 'The Bravest', are to the fore.

We ask your protection, Lord, for those who fight fires and pray that those who start fires will be made to confront the horror of their actions.

25th: It's Deaf/Blind Awareness Week, a disability described by some as the loneliest condition in the world. Never let us take our own gifts of sight and hearing for granted. We ask you, Lord, to help us to be fully aware and sensitive to the difficulties of those facing life without one or more of their senses.

26th: Today is National Music Day. We thank you, Lord, for the skill and devotion of those who compose, play, sing, teach and perform music. Listening to music can lift the spirit or bring us to tears; it can also be used to glorify your name with songs of praise. May we never be shy to make a loud noise for Our Lord.

27th: National Veterans' Day (instituted 2006). Today is the day on which we remember all those who have served this country in a military capacity.

Since the Second World War, our armed forces have been called upon to fight in Korea, Malaya, The Falklands, Northern Ireland, Afghanistan and Iraq. We give thanks that this day will ensure that the contribution they made is acknowledged and remembered.

28th: Assassination of Archduke Franz Ferdinand took place in 1914, thus beginning a conflict which lasted four years and claimed millions of lives.

We ask you, Lord, to guide all Heads of State, those people who rule our countries and our destinies, that international disagreement will be settled by negotiation and that force of arms will be used only as a last resort.

29th: The great feast of Saints Peter and Paul: St Peter, the rock upon which the Christian Church was founded, and St Paul, the Church's first great missionary. St Peter was crucified and St Paul beheaded, both martyrs for their faith.

In their names we pray for the leadership of today's church, we pray for those who are putting the word of God into action around the world and we pray for those who, even today, suffer danger or persecution because of their Christian faith.

30th: In 1960 The Belgian Congo gained independence from Belgium. This was followed by a period of terror and bloodshed for the indigenous population. We pray for all the newly independent countries of Africa that tribal and religious differences will be put aside and that people of all colours will have an equal part to play in their country's future, leading to greater justice and stability for the whole of Africa.

AND ANOTHER THING . . . .

6th: *Feast of St Norbert who was from the Rhineland - which even to this day is a Catholic stronghold in Germany. During the second World War, Cardinal von Galen, known as 'The Lion of Munster', was archbishop there. He opposed many of Hitler's policies and rotten old Adolf wanted him permanently removed but Goering and others argued that by doing so the whole of the Rhineland would be lost to the Third Reich, such was the charisma of that great churchman. Nobby Stiles, one of the 1966 World Cup heroes, was named after St Norbert – how about that?*

*On **7th** and **8th** we celebrate two English saints, St Robert of Newminster, a Cistercian who established abbeys in the N.E. of England, and William of York whose appointment as Archbishop of York was opposed by the Cistercians. He was the nephew of King Stephen who, let's be honest, didn't do a lot for the church or the country, did he?*

24th: *The Feast of the Birth of John the Baptist. I always remember this feast particularly because it's my son's birthday. I hope Rory realises how lucky he is; if he'd been born to Italian parents, he may well have been named 'Baptista'. I'm lucky too – lucky to have a son to be proud of. I hope my son knows how proud I am of him and understands why. He should do because he now has a son of his own to be proud of.*

Corpus Christi: In 1246, Bishop Robert de Thorete of Liège, convened a synod and instituted the celebration of the feast. From Liège, the celebration began to spread, and, on 8th September, 1264, Pope Urban IV established the Feast of Corpus Christi as a universal feast of the Church, to be celebrated on the Thursday following Trinity Sunday.

St Thomas Aquinas composed the office (the official prayers of the Church) for the feast. The feast was celebrated with a Eucharistic procession in which the Sacred Host was carried throughout the town, accompanied by hymns and litanies. The faithful would venerate the Body of Christ as the procession passed by.

During this time of Corpus Christi we remember that you kept your people alive in the desert by giving them food from heaven. We give thanks for the gift of the Eucharist by which you continue to provide for your people: may it serve to unite us as one body.

A THOUGHT
TO MAKE GOD SMILE

Always borrow money
from a pessimist:
he won't expect it back.

July – Saintly factoid:

St Thomas the Apostle is celebrated on the 3rd July. His legend speaks of his being chosen amongst the apostles to go to India. He introduced himself there to the ruler, King Gundafor, as a carpenter and builder. He was employed to build a palace for the king but he gave all the money to the poor. He was condemned to prison and death – but Gundafor's brother died and saw in heaven the beautiful palace built out of the alms given by Thomas to the poor. The brother returned to earth to offer to buy Gundafor's heavenly palace but the king would not sell. He then released Thomas and was baptised along with many of his subjects. If only we had built the Millennium Dome in heaven . . .

If it's snowing in July,
is Nature out to fool yer?
It's as my grandma says,
'the weather's most peculiar'.

Stewart Henderson

1st: First Day of the Somme. At 7:30 on that day, on a 14 mile front from Serre to Maricourt, 110,000 men went over the top. By mid-day 10,000 of them were dead, killed by rifle bullets, machine gun bullets and artillery shells, ours as well as theirs. At the end of the First day we had 19,240 dead, 35,493 wounded, 2,152 missing and 585 taken prisoner, a total of 57,470. The soldiers involved were a citizen's army, the result of Kitchener's 'Your Country Needs You' campaign. They were young men who had lost their fathers, old men who had lost their sons, brothers joining up together. They fostered strong motives of patriotism and revenge. There were Pals' Battalions: Manchester Pals, Sheffield Pals, Grimsby Chums, Glasgow Boys, men from the same street, the same football team, the same cycling club who all knew one another and joined up to "do their bit together". This compounded the tragedy of that July; it is said that in Accrington everyone had a friend or relative lost or wounded to the carnage of the Somme. Our country also forfeited the cream of the next generation, the men who were to have been the future captains of industry, commerce, politics, arts and culture. There are 147 war cemeteries on the Somme Battlefield: British, French and German.

The Thiepval Memorial alone bears the names of 72,000 men who have no known resting place. Lord, may that memorial and the shining white headstones which surround it serve as a reminder to politicians of all nations to strive always for peace.

2nd: William Booth established The Salvation Army in 1865.
We pray for all officers and soldiers of The Salvation Army worldwide. They are your infantry, Lord, taking up arms against poverty, homelessness, drugs, vice. Front line troops need support. Show us how to give that support, Lord, and aid them in their fight.

3rd: Feast of St Thomas the Apostle, 'Doubting Thomas'. Lord, we ask for Thomas to intercede for us when we question our faith. "Unless I see and touch, I will not believe" he said. Strengthen my belief, Lord, that without seeing or touching I will always proclaim you as "my Lord and my God".

4th: On this American Independence Day we pray that the richest and most powerful country on the globe will use its wealth and influence for the good of the world as a whole and, in these ecologically sensitive times, be aware that the resources of the world are for the use of all your children.

5th: Many people in our country now feel that the Church is out of touch with their lives. Lord, give the ministers of your church the ability to reach out to these souls that their lives may be touched by the true message of Christianity: forgiveness, salvation, truth and love.

6th: In the centre of Prague there is a large statue to John Huss. The Lutheran Church marks this date on which John Huss was burned at the stake because of his writings in criticism of the established church. We thank you, Lord, that we now live in an enlightened age where change and reformation are seen as valuable and progressive.

7th: It's the anniversary of the dreadful Tube bombings which took place in London:

For the rescue workers - police and fire officers,
paramedics, and hospital staff
we pray God's strength;
For the fellow-travellers stopping to comfort,
soothe and tend the wounds
we pray God's compassion;

For those who are dispirited,
angry, despairing, and grieving
we pray God's comfort;
For those who turn to violence
to achieve their ends
we pray God's forgiveness;
For our sisters and brothers
of all faiths and of none
we pray God's blessing;
For ourselves - numbed, fearful,
morbidly fascinated or guiltily relieved -
we pray God's light in our lives.

As we hold before God those who suffer, we give thanks for every sign of the resilience of the human spirit and the determination not to be cowed by the cowards. We pray that all people may learn to live in peace and with mutual respect.

8th: Don't bother to tell God you've got a big problem, just tell your problem that you've got a big God. "Be strong and of good courage; be not afraid, neither be thou dismayed; for the Lord thy God is with thee whithersoever thou goest." [Joshua 1:9]

9th: On this the Feast of St Augustine Zhao Rong and Companions we pray for all who brought

Christianity to China, the world's most populous country, and we ask your blessing and protection, Lord, for Christians in China today where persecution is never far below the surface.

10th: In National Transplant Week we give thanks for all those who carry a donor card by which, in the event of their death, they could give life to another; but at the same time we ask your help for those trying to put a stop to the trade in illegally harvested human organs.

11th: It's United Nations' World Population Day. As population increases, pressures on the resources of our world increase.
It's said that you, Lord, provide enough for man's need but not for man's greed. Help us to do all we can to share out the bounties you have granted us and to remember that they are for the benefit of all not just the few.

12th: End of Falklands War 1982. We pray for the proud people of this inhospitable land and we pray, too, for the people of Argentina, for friendly relations between our country and theirs, that the South Atlantic will never again become an area of conflict.

13th: We thank you, Lord, for your promise that you will always be with us. Help us to rejoice in your presence now and to look forward to the fullness of joy which is promised us in the life to come.

14th: Lord, enable me to turn from everything in my life that would keep me from living in response to the prompting of your Spirit, for only then can I truly be your disciple.

15th: The Feast of St Swithin reminds us of the damage that can result from an excess of rain and the hardships from a lack of rain.
Lord, let us never underestimate nor take for granted the power of nature.

16th: There are 21 missions on the coast of California. They were built by Spanish Franciscans and great cities - St Francisco, Santa Barbara, San Jose - have grown up around them. Today marks the foundation of the first mission, San Diego, by Fr Junipero Serra.
We give thanks for the California missions, many of which are still places of active worship, and we remember Blessed Junipero Serra and his friars who brought Christianity to the west coast of North America.

17th: School holidays have started or are about to start. We pray that parents will take the opportunity to enjoy the company of their children, giving them that most precious of all gifts - time. We ask, too, that those youngsters awaiting exam results will not let anxiety spoil their holidays and that teachers and pupils alike will use this period of renewal to ensure that they are refreshed and ready for the autumn term.

18th: Birthday of Nelson Mandela. He spoke these words in court before being imprisoned in 1964: "I have cherished the ideals of a democratic and free society in which all persons live together in harmony with equal opportunities. It is an ideal which I hope to see realised but, my Lord, if needs be it is an ideal for which I am prepared to die."
We pray for all those imprisoned for their political or religious beliefs. We pray, too, for the repose of the soul of this great statesman.

19th: An important date for Liverpool. In 1904 the building of the city's Anglican Cathedral began. It was consecrated on this day in 1924. The two cathedrals, one Anglican, one Roman Catholic, are joined by Hope Street.
We ask you, Lord, to give hope to this vibrant city and its citizens.

20th: I consider Claus von Stauffenberg to be a great hero of the Second World War. A Colonel in the German Army and a devout Christian, he decided that something must be done to put an end to the evil being perpetrated by Hitler and the Nazis. On this day in 1944, he planted a bomb intending to kill Hitler. It failed and Stauffenberg was executed that night. Prior to the assassination attempt, he confided in the Bishop of Berlin: he was desperate to know that killing a tyrant would not deny him entry into paradise when the time came.

"Absolve we beseech thee, O Lord, the soul of thy servant Claus; and whatsoever sins he may have committed in this life, do thou, in thy most merciful forgiveness, forgive."

21st: Do you remember where you were on this day in 1969 when man first set foot on the moon? I bet you do. Before they left the moon's surface, Armstrong and Aldrin held a mini communion service and received the Eucharist they had taken with them into space.

Lord, I thank you for the life you have given me through the gift of yourself in the Eucharist. May I be ever more aware of the wonder of this gift and grow in union with you and with my brothers and sisters in Christ.

22nd: It's the Feast of St Mary Magdalene, the first person to see Jesus after his resurrection. She was a true penitent. May her example lead us sinners to be sorry for our sins and, with the help of God's grace, to avoid the occasions of sin.

23rd: Lord, may I accept the trials, tribulations, sufferings of this day; in fact, whatever you have in mind for me whether I like it or not.

24th: It's National Laughter Week, and we thank you, Lord, for laughter which is said to be the best medicine: may it continue to ease our aches and pains. We thank you, too, for our sense of humour: may we enjoy this gift you have given us and never use it cruelly.

25th: The first ecumenical council of the whole church, convened at Nicaea in 325AD, closed on this date. Its lasting legacy is the Nicene Creed.
Lord, may we be confirmed in our beliefs according to the creed which has guided Christians for over sixteen centuries.

26th: Feast of St Joachim and St Anne, the parents of The Blessed Virgin Mary. The bond of love between parents and their child is immeasurable.

We pray for that love, Lord, and ask you to heal any strife that threatens to damage such relationships. May parents try to understand the pressures modern life put on their children and may children do nothing to cause their parents pain.

27th: On this day in 1953 the Korean War ended. This three year conflict resulted in the death of five million servicemen and civilians. Korea is once again flexing its muscles.

We ask you, Lord, to bring your spirit of wisdom to the governments of North Korea and the United States that every avenue will be explored to stem the growth of nuclear weapons and to maintain stability in our increasingly unstable world.

28th: Today Peru celebrates its National Day. We pray that the government will do more to solve the problem of its street children. Living unsupervised on the streets these youngsters are prey to drugs, prostitution and crime. Instead of being given help they are often hunted down like vermin. Give strength to the organisations and individuals who are working to alleviate their suffering.

29th: It's the Feast of St Martha, the sister of Lazarus and the patron saint of cooks.

Lord, we all need to eat. Each Sunday morning we are called to celebrate at your table. Let us always show true gratitude to those who provide us with food, be it earthly or spiritual.

30th: England won the World Cup in 1966. The nation as a whole was uplifted by the achievement of this England team. We think of all those involved in football at whatever level: those who play, those who train, those concerned with administration and, of course, the fans. There is much we can learn from our national game: discipline, determination, team spirit and the need to keep striving right to the end.

Give us these qualities in our own lives, Lord, as we strive for our own final goal: a place with you in your kingdom.

31st: The Feast of St Ignatius Loyola founder of the Society of Jesus or 'Jesuits'.

Let us today ponder on the words of St Ignatius;

> "What have I done for Christ,
> what am I doing for Christ;
> what will I do for Christ?"

AND ANOTHER THING . . . .

12th: *The Falklands: I went there shortly after the war ended to entertain the troops and 'The Kelpers', as the people who live there like to be called. They are a proud lot and staunchly British. They're a tough lot, too – you have to be tough to live in such an inhospitable land. The peace between Great Britain and Argentina is fragile, to say the least. Recently there have been murmurings from that country that they are once again looking to lay claim to the islands they call 'Malvinas'. Let's hope that our armed forces will never again be called upon to fight in the South Atlantic.*

25th: *Feast of St James the Apostle who is venerated at Compostela. The word means 'field of stars'. Let me tell you the significance of that. After Pentecost, the Apostles, all filled with the Holy Spirit, set out to various parts of the known world to spread the good news of Jesus Christ. St James went to Northern Spain, thus bringing Christianity to the Spanish. He then returned to Judea and was the first of the apostles to be martyred, being beheaded by order of Herod Agrippa. His head and body were taken, by ship, back to Northern Spain, housed in a* *church and venerated for many years. However, when the Moors took over most of Spain, the Apostle's remains were buried to save them from being destroyed. Ferdinand and Isabella threw the Moors out of Spain at the end of the 15th century but, by then, the locals had forgotten where they'd buried St James – shock, horror! He was missing for two hundred years but then a shepherd watching his flock by night saw a stream of stars in the sky. They appeared to touch the earth and the shepherd began to dig at the very place where the stars had touched. What did he find? You've guessed it – the bones of a body with a severed head. Those bones are now in a silver casket, for all to see, in the beautiful Cathedral. Hence the name; Santiago (St James) de (of) compo (field) stela (stars).*

A THOUGHT
TO MAKE GOD SMILE

We are here on earth
to do good unto others.
What the others are here for
I have no idea.

August – Saintly factoid:

One of the four major basilicas in Rome is called St. Mary Majors. A legend gives the ancient church the title 'Our Lady of the Snows'. The story tells of Pope Liberius having a dream on the night of 4th August in which there was a fall of snow (in Roman August!) on one of the hills of Rome. There, Our Lady wished a church to be built. That same night a senator, John, had a similar dream. On 5th August the Senator and the Pope met on the Esquiline Hill and discovered the miraculous fall of snow and there built a church. Hence the title 'Our Lady of the Snows'. A relief in the beautiful Borghese Chapel in the basilica shows the story of the legend.

We always went on holiday in August. Carworkers' Fortnight was the first two weeks and for fourteen days Birmingham was empty. It's a long way to the sea from Birmingham in any direction. Rhyl and Weston-super-Mare were the favourite destinations but we Macleans ventured further afield.

August always brings back textures: sand and woolley cossies that felt like a cross between a brillo pad and a shredded wheat, and smells: fish and chips and ozone - Ah, August!

1st: Father, I accept that you know what is best for me. Teach me to follow you in good times and in bad, knowing that whatever route you lead me it will be for my ultimate happiness.

2nd: On this day in 1492, all Jews were expelled from Spain.

It's said that you work in mysterious ways, Lord, and the Spanish diaspora meant that Jewish energy and invention was spread throughout Europe and North Africa. In recent years so many Nobel Prizes, particularly in the scientific field, have been won by Jews. We thank you for the benefits Jewish thinkers and scholars have brought to the countries which took them in.

3rd: We pray for the work of the Churches Conservation Trust that places where you have been worshipped for generations will continue to stand as a tribute to our Christian heritage.

4th: Feast of St John Vianney, patron of Parish Priests, Vicars, Pastors. Parish Priests do indeed have a great responsibility to their own flock.

We pray for all the pastors of the Church; may they pattern their lives on Christ, Our Saviour, who came in humility to call to himself the childlike of heart.

5th: Father, we pray for a revival of faith. We ask you to reawaken our spirituality and to keep us ever mindful that the worship of money and possessions will be of little use or value in the life to come.

6th: It's the Feast of the Transfiguration when Jesus went up Mount Tabor with Peter, James and John. There they saw him transformed, together with Moses and Elijah, and they heard a voice which said "This is my own dear son, with whom I am well pleased. Listen to Him" [Luke 9:26-38].

On this the Feast of the Transfiguration, when Jesus appeared in heavenly glory before his three closest disciples, fill our lives, Lord, with some of that light so that we may be dazzled anew by your power and majesty.

7th: You are the strong one who can carry me in my weakness and inadequacy. You will carry me and I shall not fall. I trust in you and I am no longer alone.

8th: It's the anniversary of the dropping of the atomic bombs on Hiroshima and Nagasaki.

We pray for all the Japanese men, women and children who perished as a result of that most indiscriminate of all weapons in 1945. We pray, too, for those British, Commonwealth and American troops who suffered unspeakably as POWs and for the countless people of many countries who endured slave labour and death. May the governments of the world learn from the mistakes of the twentieth century so that in future they will follow the way of truth not deception, of justice not violence, of love not hate. Father, we remember the words of your gospel "Blessed are the peace makers for they shall be called the children of God." [Matthew 5:9]

9th: It's the Feast of St Edith Stein. Born into an orthodox Jewish family she converted to Christianity and became a Carmelite nun, taking the name Teresa Benedicta of the Cross. She gave her life completely to God as is evidenced by her writings: "Whatever did not fit in with my plan did lie within the plan of God. I have an ever deeper and firmer belief that nothing is merely an accident when seen in the light of God, that my whole life down to the smallest detail has been marked out for me in the plan of Divine Providence and has a completely coherent meaning in God's all-seeing eyes." Edith Stein perished in the gas chambers of Auschwitz – may perpetual light shine upon her.

10th: On this day in 1876 the first ever telephone call was made. We give thanks for this wonderful invention by which we can keep in touch with those we love. May we be like ET and never put off the opportunity to 'phone home'.

11th: It's the Feast of St Clare, patron saint of TV: We pray for the wonderful invention of television which can and should be a power for good.
Be with network controllers, Lord, that they will always be aware of their responsibilities and carefully consider the moral content of their output.

12th: "An atheist is a man who has no invisible means of support."
Lord, we remember all those who have no faith that they will one day come to know you as we do.

13th: Father, often the terrible happenings in the world, the suffering we see on our TV screens, mean that I find it impossible to pray. Help all of us who find prayer difficult but, when we plead for your intervention, Lord, may we always include the words "Thy will be done".

14th: The Feast of St Maximillian Kolbe, a priest, who perished in Auschwitz having taken the place of another. "Greater love than this no man has than he lay down his life for his friends." [John 15:13]

15th: The Feast of the Assumption of the Blessed Virgin Mary. The observance of this was begun during the papacy of Leo IV (847-855) but it was not until 1950 that the dogma of the bodily assumption of Our Lady into Heaven was defined by Pope Pius XII. We remember that it is a thing unheard of that anyone ever had recourse to her protection, implored her help or sought her intercession and was left forsaken.
We thank you, Lord, that there is a Queen in heaven to intercede on our behalf with your beloved son.

16th: It's the anniversary of the day in 2005 when Brother Roger Schultz, who for sixty-five years led the Taize Community, was called from this life. The death of this truly ecumenical man touched the many people who over the years benefited from his ministry and those with whom he openly shared his deep faith.
Brother Roger was truly your servant, Lord: may he now receive his reward in your presence.

17th: This week marks the anniversary of Independence for India.

We give you thanks, Lord, for India, the world's largest democracy, and for the whole sub-continent with its plethora of languages, religions and cultures. We pray for those of its peoples living amongst us. We pray for organisations and individuals who minister to the poor, the sick and the infirm and we ask that the governments of India, Pakistan, Bangladesh and Sri Lanka, as well as governments in the developed world, will do all they can to see the lowly lifted up and the hungry filled with good things.

18th: Feast of St Helena, patron saint of divorced people. Divorce is always heartbreaking.

Lord, we ask your help for all people who find themselves in this sad position. Give your strength to concerned organisations such as 'Relate' as they work to support marriages which are in difficulties. We pray, too, for those people who because of the breakdown of a marriage now find themselves sad and alone. Bring light to their lives; let them know they have your love.

19th: Young people throughout the country have received or will shortly be receiving their exam results.

Many will be enjoying the rewards of successful study; we pray that they may use their intellect for the benefit of all. We remember, too, those who have been disappointed by their results. Help them, Lord, to look to the future with a sense of perspective, not despair.

20th: Today is VJ Day. The thoughts of veterans of the war against Japan will be filled with the faces of comrades who lie in some foreign field or beneath the Pacific Ocean.

We pray for the repose of all those on both sides who died as a result of the conflict and we pray also for those survivors who, even after many long years, cannot forgive. Show them, Lord, your healing love.

21st: On this day in 1879, fifteen individuals in the small town of Knock, Co Mayo, saw a vision of The Blessed Virgin Mary, St Joseph and St John the Evangelist. The apparition lasted for two hours. Today people travel from all over the world to visit the Knock Shrine.

This is the prayer to Our Lady of Knock: "Help me to remember that we are all pilgrims on the road to Heaven. Fill me with love and concern for my brothers and sisters in Jesus Christ. Comfort me when I am sick, lonely or depressed. Give me a greater love for Jesus in the Blessed Sacrament. Pray for me now and at the hour of my death."

22nd: We pray today for all adopted children. Here's a little poem. No-one seems to know who wrote it. I call it a poem but surely it's a prayer:

> Not flesh of my flesh nor bone of my bone
> But still miraculous, my own.
> Never forget for a single minute
> You didn't grow under my heart but in it.

23rd: UNESCO's International Day for the Remembrance of the Abolition of Slavery.
We give thanks, Lord, for the great reformers who defeated the despicable trade, together with the heartless people who profited from it. Yet, even today, slavery is still practiced in various forms. Help governments to do all they can to ensure that no person becomes the possession of another.

24th: Today is the feast day of the apostle, St Bartholomew, described as "an Israelite without guile" (the Gospel calls him 'Nathanael').
Lord, we pray that, with the help of your grace we, too, may be like St Bartholomew: unselfish, innocent and straightforward, always saying what we mean, bearing no grudge and never thinking evil of others.

25th: Feast of St Genesius, patron saint of actors and comedians. An important figure for all who entertain.

Father, we thank you for the talent you have given us, may we use it for your glory. Make us your instruments so that, like musical instruments, we may stay in tune with you. On us, in us and through us play your music – your way.

26th: The exam results are out. We pray that the successful candidates may choose their subjects for higher education wisely. We pray that those young people without academic qualifications may develop their skills so that they, too, will enjoy a fruitful future.

27th: Feast of St Monica. There are so many female saints who could have been declared patron of mothers but that role has gone to St Monica who prayed that her son, who had abandoned his faith, would return to the church. Her prayer was answered; he not only returned to the faith but became one of the most brilliant theologians of the Church – St Augustine of Hippo (whose feast is tomorrow).

Lord, many parents take delight in the fact that they have handed on the flame of faith to their own children. We ask the intercession of St Monica to bring back those who have abandoned the faith of their fathers and mothers, that they and their children will not be lost to you.

28th: "Small is the gate and narrow the road that leads to life and only a few find it." [Matthew 7:14] Father, show me the way.

29th: Beheading of John the Baptist by Herod Antipas at the behest of his step daughter, Salome, "an oath that was rashly taken and criminally kept." May we always carefully consider the consequences before committing ourselves to any promise whatsoever.

30th: The holiday season is rapidly coming to an end so we pray for all those who will be returning to a more normal routine. We pray for children returning to school: may they look forward with a positive attitude to all the fresh opportunities for learning and experience. We pray for those returning to work; may they be refreshed and prepared for challenges ahead.

31st: On the anniversary of Princess Diana's death we give thanks, Lord, for her life and the legacies she left, including her advocacy of landmine clearance. We ask your blessings, Lord, on all those who have lost limbs as a result of the indiscriminate use of landmines. We thank you for the bravery of those who risk their own lives as they attempt to locate the mines and render them safe.

AND ANOTHER THING . . . .

6th: *While an important event in Christ's life, the Transfiguration was added to the Christian calendar relatively late, and few people realize that it was not declared a universal feast of the Church until 6th August, 1456. Even fewer know that it owes its place on the calendar, in part, to the courageous actions of Dracula. Yes, Dracula - or, more precisely, Vlad III the Impaler, who is better known to history by the dreaded name. Pope Callixtus III added the Feast of the Transfiguration to the calendar to celebrate the important victory of the Hungarian nobleman Janos Hunyadi and the elderly priest St John of Capistrano at the Siege of Belgrade in July 1456.*

Breaking the siege, their troops reinforced the Christians at Belgrade, the Muslim Turks were routed, and Islam was stopped from advancing further into Europe. With the exception of St John of Capistrano, Hunyadi could find no significant allies to accompany him to Belgrade, but he did enlist the help of young prince Vlad, who agreed to guard the passes into Rumania, thus cutting off the Turks. Without his aid, the battle might not have been won. Vlad was a brutal man whose actions earned him immortality as the fictional vampire, but some Orthodox Christians venerate him as a saint for confronting the Islamic threat to Christian Europe. As we celebrate the Feast of the Transfiguration, we might at least offer a prayer for his soul.

15th: The Assumption. *On November 1, 1950, Pope Pius XII, declared that it is a dogma of the Church "that the Immaculate Mother of God, the ever Virgin Mary, having completed the course of her earthly life, was assumed body and soul into heavenly glory." Because the declaration of the dogma is so recent, many people have the impression that the Assumption is an innovation, a new idea that Pius XII made up. Nothing could be further from the truth.*

Not only was the Feast of the Assumption celebrated universally by Christians, East and West, from the sixth century up until the Reformation, but the written record of Christian belief in the Assumption of Mary goes back to the fourth century and perhaps even before that. As early as the second century, Christians had begun to venerate the bones of martyrs and saints. Yet at no time did any local Christian church claim to possess the earthly remains of the Blessed Virgin's body, nor has anyone ever claimed to have discovered her tomb.

25th: *St Genesius, patron saint of actors and comedians, is also the patron of the Catholic Associationof Performing Arts of which I'm a vice-president. He was a Roman comedian actually carrying out a mock baptism in front of the Emperor to amuse the crowd when suddenly he became aware of the reality of baptism. He became a Christian. My younger granddaughter, Cheska, always keen to be original, chose 'Genesius' as her confirmation name.*

A THOUGHT
TO MAKE GOD SMILE

Thou shalt not
weigh more than
thy fridge.

September – Saintly factoid:

We think of St Cecilia as the patron saint of music. Her legend speaks of her playing the organ ("in cantibus organis") as she peacefully awaited death by suffocation. But for centuries Pope St Gregory the Great (feast day 3rd of this month) was the patron saint of Church music, giving his name to Gregorian Chant and having attributed to him the setting up of schools to encourage the development of Church music. In the 16th century the Roman Academy of Music was set up under the patronage of St Cecilia and from then she has gradually become regarded as the patron saint of Church music.

The first Saturday of September sees the start of the Rugby Season. It's a game that we love. Rugby football has been the cement which has held together the very strong relationship which I have with my son, Rory. He now has a son of his own, Noah. I'm sure that rugby will ensure that those two are great mates as well. Noah's birthday is 2nd September while that of his cousin, Francesca, is 20th - a truly important month for me, then.

1st: 70 AD, the destruction of Jerusalem by the Romans, the Temple destroyed, its walls nothing but rubble and the Jews cast out. Despite many attempts made to purge the earth of their presence, the Jewish people have faced every challenge and lived to meet the next.

We thank you, Lord, for the resilience of your 'Chosen People' and we applaud the contributions that Jews have made and are still making for the benefit of the world in which we live.

2nd: It's the hurricane season. Every year at this time populations in and around the Caribbean are at threat from violent storms. Sadly, it's the poorest communities that suffer most. We applaud the endurance of those who have lost homes and those who have lost everything yet refuse to be dislodged. Help them, Lord, as they toil to rebuild their lives.

3rd: Today is the Feast of St Gregory the Great who sent St Augustine with forty monks to bring Christianity to England.

We give you thanks, Lord, for the Christian faith in this land, and thanks for all the great movements of the Spirit which have shown each generation the light of God. We thank you for the great cathedrals, the humble churches and meeting halls which bear witness to the continuing history of the faith, unbroken since St Gregory's day. We offer repentance for our many failures to live up to our high calling as Christians and we ask for grace that the whole Christian community may bear witness in its life, as well as its words, to the love of God.

4th: The anniversary of the Beslan massacre in 2004 when terrorism took a new and even more inhuman turn with the targeting of small children. We can imagine the fear of those little souls too young to understand why any grown-up would want to hurt them.

We pray for those who died, for those who mourn and for the survivors who will forever be haunted by the nightmare they have lived through.

5th: St Mother Teresa of Calcutta. This little nun inspired people of all nationalities and all faiths. "I am a little pencil in the hand of a writing God who is sending a love letter to the world," she said. May we honour her memory by loving one another and caring for the poor.

6th: Lord, give me strength when I am tired,
Wisdom when I am confused or uncertain
And patience when I'm angry and frustrated.

Anon.

7th: We remember all those who are housebound and cannot get to a church service on Sunday morning. Be with them, Father, in their homes and in their hearts.

8th: It's International Literacy Day. The ability to read and write, which we take for granted is sadly not available to all.   We pray for a time when everyone throughout the world will be able to express themselves with words both written and spoken.

9th: The Jesuit priest, St Peter Claver, was sent from Spain to what is now Colombia in the early 1600s. Despite opposition, he would board every slave ship as it arrived from Africa. Entering the filthy and diseased holds, he would treat, feed and minister to the terrified human cargo. He baptised an estimated 300,000 Africans, assuring them of their human dignity and God's saving love.

Lord, may we have the courage to stand up against injustice and never turn our backs on the downtrodden. May we be like Peter Claver and accept all people, regardless of colour or nationality, as our equals in your sight.

10th: We pray for all school children as they commence the new term this week, especially those who are a little nervous of what to expect from their teachers as evidenced in this prayer from young James: "Dear God, some teachers are nice and they don't shout. Please help the shouty ones to be quiet and all of them to be nice. Help us to be nice too."

11th: It's the anniversary of the day now known simply as 9/11 when thousands of lives were lost and thousands more ruined.
We pray that 'Time', the great healer, has begun to ease the grief of those still struggling to come to terms with the loss of a loved one who simply disappeared beneath the Twin Towers, leaving no trace. We pray for the three thousand children now growing up with only one parent, may they know you as their Father; and we pray for the United States of America that they will accept their responsibilities as a major power in our increasingly dangerous world, bringing justice and wisdom to all their spheres of activity.

12th: You are the strong one who can carry me in my weakness and inadequacy. You will carry me and I shall not fall. I trust in you and I am no longer alone.

13th: Let us be mindful of the way we speak to one another. James [3:8-9] wrote "the tongue is a fire; with it we bless the Lord and with it we curse men who are made in the likeness of God".

Help us, Lord, to choose our words wisely. Put kind words into our mouths and guard us against hurtful and malicious gossip.

14th: The Feast of The Triumph of the Cross. Lord, today we celebrate the fact that your beloved Son made an instrument of humiliation and death the instrument of our salvation and conquered the world, not by the sword but by the cross.

15th: Battle of Britain Day. It's many years since a few young pilots in their Hurricanes and Spitfires stood between this country and subjugation to an evil ideology.

We thank you, Lord, for those who fought in the skies during the Summer of 1940, many of whom paid with their lives for our freedom.

> "Fly on, dear boys, from this world of strife,
> on to the promised land to eternal life."
> (Inscription on the gravestone of James McCudden VC, RFC)

16th: It's the International Day for the preservation of the Ozone Layer.

Loving Lord, help us to treat your creation with respect. When our world is in despair and the way ahead is hard to follow, renew in us a sense of hope.

17th: The anniversary of the Battle of Arnhem. We remember those who gave their lives at that time and those people, military and civilian, who suffered terrible deprivation in the aftermath; but we also give thanks for the special friendship forged between Holland and Britain by what, though a military defeat, has been described as a victory for the spirit.

18th: Dementia and Alzheimer's are increasing in our community. We ask, Lord, that you will send your spirit down on all those hard pressed relatives who are caring for a loved one suffering from these heart-breaking conditions. Help the sufferers, despite their confusion, to realise they have your love and the love of those around them. We echo the prayer of the confused: "Dear Lord, I don't know who I am, I don't know what I am, I don't know where I am but please love me".

19th: At this time of year when farmers are gathering in the harvest I ask you, Lord, to bring to maturity the seeds you have sown in the field that is my heart.

20th: Today has been named as International Day of Peace by the United Nations.

We pray for all areas of long-term conflict. Spread your spirit of peace in their direction, Lord, give wisdom and patience to those involved in negotiation there. We think, too, of domestic peace: peace between husband and wife, brother and sister, parents and children, and we pray for those seeking peace within themselves that you, Father, will give them the strength to put aside all anxious thoughts and imaginings. Lord, make us all channels of your peace and bring true peace to all peoples in the world.

21st: The Feast of St Matthew. We strive to walk in the footsteps of Jesus but Matthew walked alongside Jesus, sharing in his mission and his passion.

We thank you for his gospel by which the words and works of Jesus have been revealed to us at first hand.

22nd: We pray for the work of 'The Whale and Dolphin League'. Certain countries still condone the hunting of the great marine mammals. Modern sonar equipment means that these gentle, graceful creatures have little chance of escaping agonising death at the hands of the whalers.

Lord, aid the politicians of the rest of the world and also the fearless men and women of Greenpeace as they strive to thwart a barbaric trade which threatens to empty the seas of these majestic creatures.

23rd: Many miracles have been attributed to Padre Pio whose feast day this is. Since his canonisation in 2002, people have asked him to intercede on their behalf with this prayer.

"Help me to imitate you in your sufferings from the wounds in your hands and feet and side. I unite myself with Christ Crucified and his sorrowful Mother for the salvation of souls, especially my own. May suffering lead me to a better life and enable me to atone for my sins and the sins of the world. Amen."

24th: Father, we ask your blessing on all carers, those dedicated, often hard-pressed, people who look after a husband or wife, a child or an elderly relative in their own home. Help us all, Lord, to look for opportunities to relieve the pressure on carers that are known to us. We pray, too, for all those administering and working in residential homes for the elderly. Help society and us as individuals to do all we can to care for those who have worked hard all their lives that they may not be abandoned in their twilight years.

25th: We pray for all university students as the new university year begins: for those returning to their studies, for those starting their degree courses, and for the many mature students that they will not feel out of place. Knowledge is power: help those accumulating knowledge and those imparting it in our faculties of higher education.

26th: We ask you, Lord, to help us to meet the needs of those who are disabled and to be fully aware and sensitive to their difficulties. We pray for the work of those committed to challenging disability by providing education, training and support.

27th: St Vincent de Paul dedicated his entire life to the service of the poor. It is said that there is no human suffering that he did not seek to relieve. His legacy is the Vicentian Fathers, the Daughters of Charity and the SVP Society. On this his Feast Day, we pray for those orders who care for the poor today in the name of their founder, St Vincent.

28th: Feast of St Wenceslaus who, during a time when Paganism threatened to overtake the former Czechoslovakia, set out to promote Christianity among his subjects. In our country today there is a growing movement to discredit Christianity.

Help us, Lord, to stand firm in our faith despite the onslaught of ridicule.

29th: Michaelmas. Today, the Christian church celebrates the Feast of St Michael and All Angels and so we give thanks, Lord, for all people in history and those whom we have known personally who have stood up for what is right and who have fought against evil in the world. Above all we thank you for the final victory over evil that was won on the cross. Help us to follow Christ and to continue as his faithful soldiers to the end of our lives.

30th: Give me resilience, Lord, that I may recover quickly from adversity and setbacks. Help me always to remember that today's mighty oak is just yesterday's nut that held its ground.

AND ANOTHER THING . . . .

9th: *Feast of St Osburga or Edburga as she is also known. This all sounds a bit obscure so why do I mention it? Well, firstly, because she's an English saint and we ain't got too many of those (though we're well on the way to another one now that Pope Benedict has beatified John Henry Newman) but also because, in the 8th century, Osburga was abbess of Minster in Thanet. Now that can only be Minster on the Isle of Sheppey which lies just off the north shore of Kent in the Thames estuary. Believe it or not that's where I met my wife in 1963 – I was working as a green coat at Warner's Holiday Camp there and she came on holiday with her Mom and Dad. Definitely an excuse to celebrate this feast day!*

13th: *Feast of St John Chrysostom, known as 'Golden Mouth' a much better soubriquet than that given to David Beckham, don't you think? He is one of the four great Greek doctors of the Church, a prolific writer.*

26th: *The feast of Ss Cosmos and Damian, a most attractive pair of saints, known as 'the holy moneyless ones' because they were twin brothers who practised medicine without charging fees and were eventually put to death for their faith.*

A THOUGHT TO MAKE GOD SMILE

People who want to share
their religious views with you
almost never want you
to share yours with them.

October – Saintly factoid:

St Callistus was pope in the early third century and he is remembered on 14th October. His story is extraordinary. He was a slave who set up a bank for his master, Carporphorus. It failed, and Callistus was imprisoned. He was freed but was soon rearrested and imprisoned for brawling – probably trying to recover some of the debts that had caused the bank's failure. Freed in a general amnesty he sought a position at the papal court and won the favour of Pope Zephyrinus who entrusted him to organise the Roman Christian burial grounds (the Catacombs). When Zephyrinus died Callistus was elected Pope! In disgust, the priest Hippolytus declared himself Pope and set up his court across the city – one of the many times the Catholic Church has had more than one man claiming to be Pope. (Hippolytus later repented, returned to the Church, was martyred and is recognised as a saint.)

I've got absolutely nothing to say about October; it's damp, the trees are all naked, the days are shorter and the clocks are put back. Christmas decorations and next year's calendars are appearing in the shops. At least there's panto to look forward to.

1st: It is the Feast of St Theresa of Lisieux. These are her words:

"May today there be peace within.
May you trust God that you are
exactly where you are meant to be.
May you not forget
the infinite possibilities
that are born of faith.
May you use those gifts
that you have received
and pass on the love
that has been given to you.
May you be content
knowing you are a child of God.
Let this presence settle into your bones
and allow your soul the freedom
to sing, dance, praise and love.
It is there for each and every one of us."

2nd: Feast of the Guardian Angels. Here's another prayer from another small person named Christine.

"Dear God,
I thank you for my guardian angel.
I don't know where he is, I've never seen him.
Is he a her?
I'd like to choose a name for my guardian angel?
How do I tell if it's a him or a her?
Please let me know."

3rd: Today we pray for those police officers who have lost their lives in the line of duty and for all who mourn them. We ask you, Lord, to safeguard the lives of all the brave men and women who wear the famous blue uniform on the increasingly violent streets of Great Britain.

4th: The Feast of St Francis of Assisi, the best known saint for those who love animals, focuses our attention on the fact that animals are suffering often because of our selfish actions.
Help us, Lord, to realise that mistreatment of any creature is an offence to you and we shall one day be held to account for it. We give you thanks, Lord, for the joy that people, particularly lonely people, get from their pets.

5th: United Nations International Teachers Day. Help teachers to be conscientious and fully committed to their vocation. Help, particularly, those who feel they have been let down by a system which makes it difficult for them to maintain the discipline necessary to do their job. We pray for a situation where parents and teachers will pool their efforts in a common goal, to help each and every child reach its full potential.

6th: William Tyndale was executed in 1536. We thank you, Lord, for those who, centuries ago, translated the bible into our language, knowing the benefits we would receive from it. We pray for your servants who are now translating it into many more languages and using technology - video, film, DVD - as new ways of spreading your word. May this be of lasting benefit to all.

7th: Out of your great love you lifted me up, placed my foot on a sturdy rock. I firmly believe, Lord, that you are the firm base on which I can build my life.

8th: On World Hospice Day we thank you, Lord, for the wonderful work of the hospice movement.

We ask your blessing on all who are suffering with terminal illness. Let them feel your presence, Lord. We ask also that you will stand with their relatives and friends as they struggle to hide their anxieties from their loved one. Comfort them, Father, in their darkest days.

9th: The People's Republic of China celebrates its anniversary this week.
We pray for the people of this vast and populous country. We pray that their leaders will listen to world opinion concerning human rights and we think particularly of all Christians within China who risk persecution, even death, by practicing their faith.

10th: Today we think of deaf people. Never let us take our own gift of hearing for granted.
We ask you, Lord, to help us to meet the needs of deaf people, to be fully aware and sensitive to their difficulties. We think especially today of those committed to teaching and learning sign language in order to make life easier for those with impaired hearing.

11th: Now that the political party conference season is over we pray for our parliament and our democracy. May all those who represent us in government constantly strive to govern with honesty and compassion, bringing justice to the oppressed and help to the needy.

12th: It's the anniversary of the Bali bombing when, in 2002, so many fine young lives, full of promise, were lost to an indiscriminate act. At the subsequent trial, the parents of the victims, still in the darkest hours of mourning, asked that mercy be shown to the man who had taken from them all that they held precious.

May their compassion soften the hearts of those who, even now, plan to bring yet more terror to the world.

13th: In 539 BC Babylon was overthrown by the Persian King Cyrus, freeing the Jews from slavery and allowing them to return to their homeland. In parts of the world today people are still enslaved.

Give your strength, Lord, to those who seek to bring freedom to the oppressed.

14th: Feast of St Teresa of Avila. Lord, St Teresa sought oneness with you through contemplation and prayer; she experienced the mystical piercing of her heart by the spear of divine love. Let us, too, strive to be at one with you and experience your divine love.

15th: On this day in 1949 Billy Graham began his ministry. Through his crusades he has won millions of souls for Christianity. We give thanks for this charismatic preacher who has always been a man of great integrity and a model of moral accountability.

16th: United Nations World Food Day. Many countries in Africa still do not have sufficient food or enough money to develop their agriculture.

Lord, in your mercy pour your spirit upon all the starving people of the world. Save the wretched and give strength to the aid workers, doctors and missionaries who struggle to help those who have nothing. We pray that governments and those involved in internal conflict will face up to the true enemy – poverty.

17th: On this day in 1979, St Mother Teresa of Calcutta was awarded The Nobel Peace Prize.

We give thanks for this nun who inspired Christians throughout the world with her tireless work for the poor, the sick and the dying. We ask you to accept from us the words St Mother Teresa prayed everyday: "I love you, God, I trust you, I believe in you, I need you now."

18th: It's the Feast of St Luke. We thank you for his gospel giving us a full account of the life of

Jesus, our saviour. Enable us, Lord, to grow in knowledge of all four gospels, open our hearts to their true meaning that we may be Christlike in our everyday lives.

19th: May I recognise your presence in my life, Lord, and deepen my understanding of your loving care for me. It is your path that I seek to follow, may the Holy Spirit guide me on my way.

20th: It's National Parents' Week and we ask your blessing, Lord, on all parents that they will take pride in the vocation you have given them. Guide them in the discipline and development of the children you have entrusted to their care that they may grow up with a love of their neighbours, a concern for their world and a desire to put their trust in you.

21st: We celebrate the Battle of Trafalgar and remember the death of Lord Nelson.
We give thanks, Lord, for the sailors of the Royal Navy who throughout history have protected this nation's shores both on and under the surface of the sea. We ask your blessings upon all sailors and ask you to be with them through storm and calm, protecting them as they sail your mighty oceans.

22nd: We bring before you, Lord, the anxieties which can permeate our daily lives, particularly if we have responsibility for children, to feed them, clothe them and guide their minds. The influences on children seem so often beyond our control but we ask for wisdom in all our choices and ask that you keep the lives of our children in the palm of your hand.

23rd: I often fly over Edgehill which is very near to Wellesbourne airfield. The Battle of Edgehill was fought in 1642 during the early part of the English Civil War. This was General Astley's prayer immediately before battle commenced.

"O Lord, thou knowest how busy I must be this day; if I forget thee, do not thou forget me."

24th: Today is the anniversary of the Hungarian Uprising of 1956. This was savagely suppressed by Soviet tanks and troops.

We pray for the proud people of Hungary that, in the post Communist era, enterprise and Christianity will flourish again.

25th: The day on which six hundred lancers and horses of the famous Light Brigade rode into the Valley of Death reminds us of the terrible mistakes made in war. Recent conflicts have brought us a new phrase; 'friendly fire'. We pray for the repose of all armed forces personnel who have forfeited their lives to the blunders of others.

26th: In Geneva on this date in 1863, the world wide Red Cross was instituted. We give thanks for this institution which has comforted those injured in war, campaigned for decent treatment of prisoners of war and, in peacetime, sent aid and medical relief to wherever there is disease, poverty and famine.

27th: We pray for those people who are no longer working, simply because they are past a certain age. Their hope is that government and captains of industry and commerce may seek to create new job opportunities and that our society will not undervalue the skills and human resources that temporarily lie dormant.

28th: Feast of St Jude. Having prayed long and hard for something to no effect my mother may well have been heard to say "There's nothing for it, it'll have to be Jude." "Not Jude, surely," would come the cry from my aunts. "He's all that's left now," Mom would reply.

We thank you, Lord, that in our deepest despair when at our lowest ebb we can call upon the intercession of St Jude, the patron of desperate situations or needs. If I am ever in desperate straits, Lord, I know that Jude will bring my plea before you.

29th: Am I ready to do your work, Lord, or am I too attached to wealth and possessions? I think of Simon Peter and his brother, Andrew, of James and John, the sons of Zebedee, who when Jesus called "straightway left their nets and followed him". May I be like those fishermen of Galilee and follow you without question.

30th: So many Christians struggle with forgiveness yet the will to forgive is an important part of being a Christian.
Give us then, Lord, strength to say the word that heals and to do the deed that mends. Let us truly mean the words we say daily "we forgive those who trespass against us" that you in turn, Lord, will forgive us our transgressions.

31st: It's All Hallows' Eve when we prepare to celebrate those who have been 'hallowed' - declared holy. Grant to us, Lord, the same faith and power of love that, as we rejoice in the triumph of the saints, we may be inspired to follow their example.

AND ANOTHER THING . . . .

1st: *It's the International Day for Older Persons. Always remember that Time is a great healer but a lousy beautician.*

6th: *Feast of St Bruno - not, as you may think, the patron saint of pipe smokers and dogs with brandy barrels round their necks but, rather, the founder of the Carthusian Order. Born in Cologne in the 11th century, he studied in Rheims where the people wanted him to become their bishop but he was determined to lead the life of a hermit and went on to embrace a life of poverty, manual work, prayer and transcribing manuscripts, which became the Carthusian way of life.*

14th: *Feast of St Teresa of Avila. She founded a convent. Her nuns, many of whom were from noble Spanish families, followed the primitive Carmelite rule. They were known as 'Carmeitas Descalzas' which means shoeless. How many women do you know who are addicted to shoes? Many modern ladies would rather follow Imelda Marcos than St Teresa.*

16th: *The Feast of St Hedwig. The Roman Catholic Cathedral in Berlin is dedicated to her. From 1933-1945, Conrad von Preysing was resident at the Cathedral as Bishop of Berlin. A great man, he opposed the Nazi regime totally and lived to tell the tale. After the war he was created a Cardinal by Pope Pius XII.*

A THOUGHT
TO MAKE GOD SMILE

Tact is -
the gift of describing others
as they see themselves.

November – Saintly factoid:

All Saints/All Souls. In 610 AD Pope Boniface IV dedicated the Pantheon in Rome as a church under the title 'Our Lady and All Martyrs'. Here were kept the remains of the martyrs which had been brought for safe keeping from the Catacombs. This is the origin of the feast of All Saints – the day when the Church prays in union with all those who lived good lives: such prayer is called the Communion of Saints. In England we call warm November weather 'All Hallow's Summer' or 'Indian Summer' – just as an old saying was 'St. Luke's Summer' when warm days began in mid-October (St. Luke's feast day is 18th October).

> *No birds,*
> *No bees,*
> *No flowers,*
> *No trees –*
> *No vember!*

Thomas Hood
(1799 – 1845)

1st: It's the great Feast of All Saints. Many of us derive great inspiration from the lives of the saints or from one saint in particular. Let's remember those people who have brought inspiration into our lives - be they canonised saints, teachers, clergymen, nuns, doctors or just simple Christians: that by following their example we may inspire others as they have inspired us.

2nd: It's the Feast of All Souls, when we think particularly of those loved ones who have gone before us and of all who sleep in Christ.

May the perfect sacrifice of your son free them from the power of death and give them eternal life. Let perpetual light shine upon them that they may enjoy the vision of your glory forever.

3rd: The Feast of St Martin de Porres. Rejected by his father because of his colour, Martin has become the patron saint of inter-racial harmony.

You told us, Heavenly Father, that the greatest of all commandments is to love one another. Help each of us never to despise another human being for his colour, creed or nationality.

4th: We pray for all who find this time of year a bit heavy, people who are despondent, who feel that the challenges they face are too difficult.

Lord, pour on them your compassion that they may find comfort from the light of your truth shining in the gloom of their lives.

5th: Tonight people all over Great Britain will join together for bonfire parties.

We pray that the festivities will not be spoiled by firework accidents, that common sense will prevail and we think, too, of the many animals for whom bonfire night is a night of fear.

6th: In National Adoption Week, we pray for everyone involved in adoption. We pray for the children that they will have the chance of a stable, rich family life. We pray for the birth parents who for various reasons are unable to look after their own children and we pray for adoptive and foster parents who have opened up their hearts and lives in order to provide homes for children who need them.

Give us the gifts of compassion, courage and good judgement as we work together to promote the well being of our children.

7th: The Bolshevik Revolution began on this day in 1917. The Communist Regime with all its repression is now a thing of the past.

We pray for the new order that has emerged in this vast country. May it keep the welfare of the ordinary Russian people at heart and be no threat to world peace. We pray, Father, that control of this great country will never fall into the wrong hands.

8th: After Gordon Wilson's daughter was killed by an IRA bomb at Eniskillen, on this date, he said "I shall pray for those people tonight and every night." I feel great humility, Lord, that Gordon showed such deep Christian forgiveness in the face of grief. Bless those peacemakers who build bridges of hope and reconciliation where human nature has brought about suffering and discord.

9th: In 1938, terror attacks were made on Jewish synagogues in Berlin. This has become known as 'The Night of Broken Glass' or 'Kristallnacht'. In parts of Europe anti-semitism, sadly, still simmers. Lord, we thank you for the Jewish people and their ancient faith to which all Christians are indebted. Keep them safe from insult or attack and keep the minds of Jews and gentiles alike free from the poison of prejudice.

10th: The anniversary of the fall of the Berlin Wall. We ask your blessings, Lord, on the people of the reunified Germany. We pray for all the countries which for many years were separated from us by the Iron Curtain. May the new order which has since been created be more productive than the one they have left behind and may there be no threat to peace in the region.

11th: Feast of St Martin de Tours, a 4th Century Roman soldier. One day during a very hard winter he chanced upon a poor man, nearly naked, begging at the gates of Amiens. Having no money to give, Martin drew his sword, cut his cloak in two and gave half of it to the beggar. The following night Christ appeared to him in a vision, wearing the half cloak and said "Martin clothed me with this garment."
Lord, instil within me the belief that acts of charity are a duty not an option. Let me never hesitate to share what I have with those less fortunate than myself.

12th: We ask your protection, Lord, for all the emergency services: paramedics, firemen, police, ambulance, coastguards, etc., and all those who are there at moments of tragedy and extreme danger.

May they be well served by their equipment, thus enabling them to react as quickly as possible to prevent suffering and save human lives.

13th: Chad Varah founded the Samaritans in 1953. We ask your blessing, Father, on that organisation and on all volunteers and counsellors who have the special skills and tender hearts to listen to people in trouble. We pray, Lord, for those who feel alone, for all who are disturbed or anxious: be to them a light in their darkness, refuge and strength in times of fear. Give hope to all your children that they will never be driven to contemplate ending their own lives.

14th: It is Prince Charles' birthday today.
We pray for our future sovereign. Bless him with your spirit of wisdom, Lord, that any decisions he makes now and in the future will be made with courage, integrity and honour. We pray, too, for our Queen who, like any other mother, has the welfare of her children and grandchildren at heart.

15th: We pray today for the many practitioners of the Muslim faith who live amongst us. As an Abrahamic religion Islam shares common ground with Christianity and Judaism.

May we welcome Muslims who attempt to explain their faith to us and, in the process, remove from our minds prejudice and misunderstanding.

16th: On International Day of Tolerance, help me, Lord, to do all I can to make this country and this world a place of tolerance and peace.

17th: We pray for those who have been killed on our roads and for those who grieve their loss. We remember also all who have been injured in body and mind and those who care for them.

Loving God, use us as we are able, to comfort and support those who suffer and what we cannot do for them be pleased yourself to do so that in the mystery of your love they may find peace and healing.

18th: On this day in 1991, Terry Waite was released after four-and-a-half years as a hostage.

We thank you, Lord, for this proof of the power of prayer, proof that hope in you is never misplaced. We thank you, too, for yellow ribbons; may they continue to remind us that there are many hostages throughout the world, a few whose names we know, most whom we may never even hear of.

Grant them freedom, Lord: may they be restored to the arms of their loved ones. Pour your love on the hostage takers, open their eyes that they realise their evil ways and, through your grace, relinquish them.

19th: On this day in 1863 President Abraham Lincoln delivered the Gettysburg address. We echo the words contained in that famous speech and pray "that government of the people, by the people, for the people, shall not perish from the earth."

20th: Today is Universal Children's Day.
Father, your son was brought up in a human family. We pray today for all children throughout the world: for those who look after them, teach them, guide them and set them an example of how to live. Give these people the courage to stand up for what is morally right. Help us all to cherish the innocence of youth and to take seriously our responsibilities as adults, that the earth may be filled with your glory by and for the next generation.

21st: On this day in 1974, the IRA bombed Birmingham. A lad who lived in the house directly opposite mine and who went to the same primary school as me was one of the twenty-one victims.

There are still people prepared to fight in Northern Ireland: they are not the men of violence but the warriors for peace, determined to go into battle, if necessary, to ensure that their province is never again split by religious conflict.

Give them strength, Lord, and let common sense prevail.

22nd: Feast of St Cecilia, patron saint of music. We thank you, Lord, for the gift of music, for those who play it, sing it or compose it. Help us to appreciate what a powerful a gift it is. May we never miss an opportunity of using it to praise you and spread your word.

23rd: Lord, let all my dreams be sweet dreams. To have a dream is a gift directly from you, a sign that there is a possibility beyond the immediate needs of daily life. To live a dream come true is also a gift from a loving God, a cause for thanksgiving and a song in the heart.

24th: On this day in 1572, the Scottish Protestant reformer, John Knox, died. In his famous book 'The Monstrous Regiment of Women' he said: "To promote a woman to bear rule, superiority, dominion or empire above any realm, nation or city is repugnant to nature." He'd get a bit of a shock if he was about now, wouldn't he?

Lord, we give thanks that women have brought a new dimension to areas which have previously been in the male domain: commerce, industry, the military and particularly the Church. We pray for every female minister of religion who has endured hardship and prejudice to pursue her vocation. Give each of them your blessing, Lord, as they do your work and tend to the flock you have entrusted to them.

25th: In 1990 Lech Walensa became President of Poland. We pray for the people of Poland, many of whom have recently come to this country, that their deeply held religious beliefs will serve to start a revival of Christianity here.

26th: We pray for the youth of the world. The opportunities for young people have never been greater, yet neither have the stress levels. The expectations of parents, teachers, sports coaches can stifle the ability to just enjoy life. We pray, Lord, for all young people who are trying to live their lives through you and we ask you to enlighten the older generation to the problems of those growing up, such as peer pressure and the need to conform. Give us understanding and compassion, Lord.

27th: In 1095 Pope Urban II proclaimed the first crusade to recapture Jerusalem.

We pray for the Holy City which is so important to Jews, Muslims and Christians. Give us hope that historical hatred can be put aside and that people of all nationalities and all faiths will, in future, share Jerusalem and all its Holy places in peace.

28th: On this day in 1968 Enid Blyton was called to her eternal reward. Her books, over six hundred of them, have shaped the minds of children for many decades.

Surely one of your greatest gifts, Lord, is the ability to write. Open a book and we are transported to countries, even other worlds, which we could never otherwise visit. We thank you for the gift you gave to Enid Blyton and further thank you that she shared that gift with all of us.

29th: 1530. Death of Cardinal Thomas Wolsey, who, shortly before he died, said: "If I had served God as diligently as I have done the king, he would not have given me over in my grey hairs."

Lord, let me never, even in my darkest days, lose faith in you for you are my salvation, the stronghold of my life.

30th: The Feast of St Andrew, patron of Scotland. We thank you, Lord, for the rugged beauty of Scotland, its highlands, its lowlands and its vibrant cities. We thank you for the Scottish people who can be found in every part of the world, those who have taken the pipes, the tartan and the Christian faith to many a distant shore. May the passionate belief they have in themselves and in you continue to thrive in the great cathedrals and lowly chapels of this historic land.

AND ANOTHER THING . . . .

15th: *The Feast of St Albert the Great. Known as 'The Universal Teacher' he was one of the greatest minds of all time. He it was who taught Thomas Aquinas. Physics, astronomy, chemistry, biology, physiology, geography, geology and botany, all came under his sphere of scholarship. He was canonised and declared a doctor of the church in 1931. He is the patron saint of students of natural sciences.*

25th: *The feast of St Catherine of Alexandria. Her legend is quite ridiculous and very bloodthirsty – I love it! She was a beautiful, high-born woman who confronted the Emperor Maxentius for worshipping idols. Fifty philosophers were brought in but she demolished their arguments and they were burnt alive for their failure. The Emperor wanted to marry her but she refused to deny her faith. She was strapped to a spiked wheel and rolled down hill but the wheel shattered. She survived but several spectators were killed by flying splinters [the death toll rises]. Her survival brought about the conversion of 200 soldiers who were immediately beheaded [the bodies are really piling up now]. Finally Catherine was beheaded too and, guess what, from her severed veins flowed not blood but milk. There's no real proof that she ever existed but it all does go to prove that you should never let the truth interfere with a good story.*

A THOUGHT TO MAKE GOD SMILE

Four stages of life:

You believe in
Father Christmas;
You don't believe in
Father Christmas;
You are
Father Christmas;
You look like
Father Christmas.

December – Saintly factoid:

On 28th December 1940 the city of London suffered a heavy bombing raid from German war planes in the area around St. Paul's Cathedral. Paternoster Row, Amen Corner and much of Ave Maria Lane were destroyed. The names recall the medieval Corpus Christi processions held around St. Paul's – the prayer timed to suit the actual route: the 'Our Father' in Paternoster Row, 'Amen' as they turned the corner into Ave Maria Lane which began the 'Hail Mary' and on to Creed Lane and the recitation of the 'I Believe.'

December, the season of good will to all men so -

May your neighbours respect you,
Trouble neglect you,
The angels protect you
And Heaven accept you.

1st: Today is World Aids Day. The United Nations have said that the fight against Aids is the greatest challenge to our age and generation. Our thoughts are drawn to the terrible suffering of Aids victims in Africa. We pray for the decimated communities, for the babies born with Aids and for the millions of orphaned children.

Lord, pour down your spirit of wisdom on medical scientists striving to find a cure and when that cure is found let it be available to those in most need. We pray for victims of the HIV virus in this country, for those nursing them and for their families that they may find it in their hearts to continue to offer support.

2nd: St Paul's Cathedral opened in 1697.

We ask your continued blessing on this great cathedral which stood as a beacon of defiance for Londoners during the blitz and on all the majestic cathedrals and humble churches of our land that they may stand as beacons of your love to the entire country.

3rd: We pray for migrants, all those who have fled their homeland whatever the circumstances. Give us the ability and the will to welcome those who seek sanctuary in our country.

4th: On a visit to Rome in 2005, I made a point of going into the crypt and offering a prayer at the tomb of the only English Pope, Adrian IV, who was elected to the Papal Throne on this day in 1154.
Lord, I thank you that a countryman of mine has been the Vicar of Christ, your representative here on earth.

5th: Let us do all we can to treat others with dignity, especially those in their twilight years, and may we always endeavour to be worthy of the honour and respect paid by others to us.

6th: It's Plain English Week, a week in which to cast aside circumlocution and verbiage and replace them with words we can understand like 'waffle'.
We give thanks for the English language which has more words than any other. Let us never use it to display our superiority over anyone else.

7th: It's the anniversary of the Roman Catholic and Greek Orthodox Church's reconciliation after a split which lasted nine hundred years.
Lord, we thank you for sending your Holy Spirit to inspire your Church. Help us to conquer our pride and overcome the many barriers we have erected that all denominations may go forward into the twenty-first century under one banner as 'Christians'.

8th: The Feast of The Immaculate Conception. When I am alone, lost and without hope, I can always turn to Mary for she understands my problems in a more profound way than I could imagine.

Jesus, you have given me an indescribable gift, your own Mother as my Mother. May I never lose sight of the fact that she prays for me "now and at the hour of my death."

9th: About this time followers of the Jewish faith are celebrating Hanukah, the festival of light.

May we, Lord, join with our Jewish brothers and sisters and increase our light to dispel the darkness of the world.

10th: On Human Rights Day, we bring before you, Lord, all those who suffer cruelty and oppression, those who live in fear, those who are afraid to speak out. Grant them hope in your justice, faith in your power to save and knowledge of your love. Turn the hearts of those who oppress the weak that they may see themselves in those they hurt and acknowledge their own need for forgiveness.

11th: We pray for the troubled, once bountiful, country of Zimbabwe which on this day in 1979 gained its independence from Great Britain.

We think of all its people, many of whom are in fear of their lives. The plight of the white farmers has become ever more dangerous. Grant them your protection, Lord, that having lost their land and their possessions they find a haven safe from physical harm.

12th: On this day in 1712 the USA passed the Sunday Law by which all persons were obliged to attend church, refrain from skilled labour and do no travelling by horse or wagon. A tad severe you might think but current legislation has deprived us of our Sunday.

Father, you set aside a day on which we could rest and think of you. It is becoming increasingly difficult to keep Sunday special. We pray that people may still find a way to build space in their lives for prayer, for recreation and for one another and that, in spite of economic pressures, we will still be able to keep sight of the ultimate importance of spiritual values.

13th: It's the Feast of St Lucy who is the patron of those with eyesight problems. In this county there are one million blind or partially sighted people.

We ask you, Lord, to help us to meet the needs of blind people: to be fully aware and sensitive to their difficulties. We especially think of those who are coming to terms with blindness for the first time. We pray for the work of such organisations as RNIB, committed to challenging blindness by providing education, training and support.

14th: Toc H chartered on this day. It was started by Tubby Clayton, a padre or army chaplain. During the First World War he took possession of a house in Poperinge, a few miles behind the British front-line trenches at 'Wipers'. His intention was to have a place where men who had been in battle and would shortly again be, could relax from the horrors of war. With that in mind, over the doorway he put a sign "Abandon rank all ye who enter here".

Lord, we thank you that, in your eyes, all men are equal and that when we finally stand before you, rank, medals, qualifications and social standing will have no bearing on your opinion of us.

15th: Walt Disney died on this day in 1966. The legacy he left behind means that, no matter how old we are, Walt's imagination can easily return us to our childhood.

Lord, keep me ever mindful that "growing old is inevitable but growing up is optional".

16th: In 1689 The Bill of Rights was passed, imposing many restrictions on Roman Catholics. These were to remain in place until The Catholic Empancipation Act was passed in 1829.

We pray that people within these British Isles will never again be discriminated against for reasons of religious belief.

17th: Wright Bros Day in United States marks the first flight by a heavier-than-air machine. The modest dream of Orville and Wilbur was to leave the surface of the earth and fly; a mere sixty-six years later, man flew to the moon.

We thank you, Lord, for all the great inventions but ask you to keep us from believing that by ourselves we have invented anything at all.

18th: Choirs have been practicing harder than ever for the wonderful carol services we so enjoy at this time of year.

We give you thanks for the skill and devotion of choir leaders who spend hours blending voices and co-ordinating movements so that individuals become one body praising, spreading your word through song.

19th: May you, Father, bless children everywhere and fill their hearts and lives with the sunshine of your love.   May they touch many adult hearts, melting them into being evermore loving, evermore caring, evermore giving individuals.

20th: Many people will be praying for snow to make the Christmas season complete.
I ask you, Lord, to cover my faults as snow covers the earth and shower me with your goodness as trees are showered with snow.

21st: It's Forefathers' Day in the USA; the anniversary of the day on which one hundred and three pilgrims landed at Plymouth Rock. Even today people feel compelled, as the Mayflower pilgrims did, to leave their own country and seek freedom of worship which is denied to them at home.
Lord, give us tolerance towards those whose beliefs and practices differ from our own that everyone may practice their own faith without fear of intimidation or abuse.

22nd: In 1216 Pope Honorius III officially approved 'The Order of Preachers' or 'Dominicans'. We give thanks for the preachers, thinkers and missionaries who through it have dedicated their lives to your service.

23rd: It is the anniversary of Ireland's being partitioned. Surely no-one could have foreseen the horror this would bring to the North in recent years. We pray for all the citizens of Northern Ireland who lived in the shadow of the bomb and the bullet for far too long.

Lord, you have promised the ultimate triumph of good over evil: may both Catholic and Protestant communities remain committed to peace and to bringing glory to your name.

24th: We think of those seeking shelter as Mary and Joseph did on the first Christmas Eve. We pray for organisations and individuals in our country who work so hard to relieve the plight of the homeless. We ask you, Lord, to give us the will to help if we are able.

25th: On this the birthday of Our Beloved Saviour, we pray that we will carry Jesus with us throughout our lives so that, just as Mary brought him to the world, we may bring him to others.

26th: Today is the feast of St Stephen, the first Christian martyr, a man "full of faith and power" who called his accusers "stiff-necked men".

Lord, keep our necks supple, enable us to turn our heads to see what is happening around us, where we have been as well as where we are going.

27th: On this day in 2004 we all learned a new word 'Tsunami' – fearsome wave. I can think only of psalm 46: "God is our refuge and strength, a very present help in trouble. Therefore shall we not fear, though the earth be removed and mountains be carried into the midst of the sea."

28th: Feast of the Holy Innocents, victims of Herod's genocide. We pray for the innocents in today's world: the starving children of Africa, the street children of South America.

Here at home we read regularly of babies and very small children killed in their own homes by neglect or physical abuse.

Lord, help us and governments to do all we can to protect the innocents.

29th: Today is the Feast of the Holy Family. We pray for all parents; help them that by example they will teach their children to know and love you, Lord, and to lead a Christian life.

30th: The New Year is almost upon us . . .
As we look back on this last year help us to realise that you are with us at all times, Lord, and that every year of our lives is a gift from you. We give you thanks for the gift of life.

31st: Thank you, Lord, for all you did for me during this year and all that you intend to do for me in the year to come.

AND ANOTHER THING . . . .

1st: *Feast of St Edmund Campion. He was a young priest executed during the reign of Elizabeth I for saying mass in England. He is one of the 40 recognised English martyrs.*

3rd: *Feast day of St Francis Xavier. With St Ignatius Loyola and 5 others he founded The Society of Jesus or Jesuits. He took the Christian faith to India and to Japan. He was proclaimed patron of all foreign missions by Pope Pius X.*

A THOUGHT
TO MAKE GOD SMILE

Don't wait
for six strong men
to take you to church.

Sunday Celebrations

Sunday is the Lord's Day, the day after the Sabbath Day, and early Christians even called it the Eighth Day! They celebrated the Word of God in the synagogue with their brothers and sisters of Israel on the Sabbath Day, and then gathered for the Breaking of Bread, the Eucharist, on the following day - which came to be called 'The Lord's Day'.

Sundays are thus always special and the Christian community has come to choose themes for prayer and celebration for many Sundays in the course of the year.

In the following section many of the best known celebrations, familiar to church-goers and non church-goers alike, are mentioned, and the prayers draw the whole community together - as they did in the 'Good Morning Sunday' programme every week for fifteen years.

Sundays are listed in the order they are encountered during the year: months given are only guides, as days are sometimes dependent on other dates.

BAPTISM OF THE LORD *(January)*

On this the Feast of the Baptism of the Lord, when the Holy Spirit descended upon Jesus as he was baptised in the Jordan, revealing to the world that he was truly your son, we ask you to keep us who were also born of water and the spirit faithful to our Christian calling that we may one day hear you say "You are my children in whom I am well pleased."

HOMELESSNESS SUNDAY *(January)*

At this time of low temperatures and the possibility of ice and snow, homeless people, already at risk in so many ways, are in even more danger of dying of exposure. Jesus said "The poor will be with you always." Help us not to treat that as a fact we can do nothing about and may those agencies who seek to help the homeless be given the resources to carry out their essential work.

DAY OF PRAYER FOR REFUGEES *(January)*

We pray for all those who have fled their own country, whatever the circumstances. Give us the ability and the will, Lord, to welcome those who seek sanctuary in our country.

(The United Nations observe World Refugee Day on 20th June)

EDUCATION SUNDAY *(February)*

It is Education Sunday, the day on which we are asked to pray for students and teachers. So often we hear the phrase "If only I had my schooldays over again."

Lord, help our young people to enjoy and benefit from their schooling, it only comes round once. Help teachers to be conscientious and truly committed to their vocation. May those formulating education policy never overlook the importance of Religious Education in the curriculum. And we pray especially for church schools, the places where the faith of the next generation is nurtured. Guide and protect all who teach and learn in them, Lord.

DAY OF PRAYER
FOR THE UNEMPLOYED *(February)*

We think particularly today of those people of all ages who, for one reason or another, have no job. We ask your blessing on them all that they may be given courage and confidence to pursue employment. And help those of us in employment to show true understanding of the plight of the unemployed that they may maintain their self-respect.

FIRST SUNDAY OF LENT *(February/March)*

This week sees the start of the season of Lent in which Christians prepare for the events of Easter. Some will give up things for the season but, whether or not we do make personal sacrifice, may we remember how much you, Lord, gave up for us: your only son, Jesus Christ.

SECOND SUNDAY OF LENT *(March)*

It's the second Sunday of the season of Lent, a time of fasting and reflection. Lord, as we struggle with our own forty days in the wilderness, give us the discipline to resist temptation and by so doing come closer to you.

THIRD SUNDAY OF LENT *(March)*

As we continue in the season of Lent we think of the suffering of your son, Jesus Christ, on our behalf and know that whenever and wherever there is pain or hardship or oppression you are there and your love is constant.

'MOTHERING SUNDAY'
FOURTH SUNDAY OF LENT *(March)*

A truly joyous day, but I always remember the first Mothers' Day after I lost my Mom; shops full of cards and I didn't have to buy one any more – that was a real blow.

On Mothering Sunday we remember Mary, the mother of Jesus, who stood at the foot of the cross on which her beloved son died. May her love be an inspiration and comfort to all mothers who have suffered the loss of a child.

Most of us first learned about you, Lord, from our own mothers. Grant that all mothers will bring up their children with a knowledge of the love of God and by example lead them along the path of Christ.

We pray for family stability, we pray for working mothers and we pray for the increasing numbers of mothers who for one reason or another are bringing up a family on their own. Give them your strength, Lord, and help us to show love and understanding.

Finally, Lord, we remember all those who no longer have mothers to buy cards for on this day. Comfort them in the knowledge that their mothers are safe in your care.

FIFTH SUNDAY OF LENT *(March)*

As our Lenten journey reaches Passion Sunday, the day on which Jesus looked towards Jerusalem knowing the terrible suffering and death that awaited him, we ask you, Lord, to deepen our faith and understanding of this holy season that we may more fully participate in Christ's journey to the cross, his death and glorious resurrection on Easter Day.

PALM/PASSION SUNDAY *(March/April)*

On Palm Sunday, we celebrate the day on which your beloved son rode in triumph into Jerusalem. Let us be ever mindful of the promise that Christ will come again in triumph. Prepare us for that moment, Lord.

EASTER DAY *(April)*

At Easter, we focus on the joy of the Resurrection and the power of what Jesus achieved in dying on the cross as our Saviour. Help us to always be aware in our hearts that 'Christ the Lord is risen today!'

THE LONDON MARATHON (April)

Thousands of runners will today compete in this year's London marathon, giving their all to raise millions of pounds for deserving charities. Encourage all those who are prepared to make sacrifices for the benefit of others, bless their efforts, give them the strength to keep going all the way to the finish and may the money raised be used wisely to enhance the lives of those in need.

> *"Dear Lord, I praise you,*
> *I thank you,*
> *I ask for your blessings."*
> Prayer of St Bernard

LOW SUNDAY (April)

Today we think of 'Doubting Thomas' and Christ's return to convince him. May we be aware that in every believer there is doubt as well as faith. We pray that we shall not feel guilty when we doubt but that our seeking and questioning will serve to strengthen and deepen our faith.

DIVINE MERCY SUNDAY *(April)*

Today is a relatively new day in the Christian calendar. Dedicated to Sister Faustina Kowalska, a Polish nun to whom Jesus appeared in visions, it is a day for penance and forgiveness of sins and a day on which people who have fallen away from church would be encouraged to return.

Lord, may we never miss the opportunity to bring a lapsed Christian back into your fold. We thank those who have helped us to be steady in the faith.

> *"Lord Jesus Christ, Son of God,*
> *have mercy on me, a sinner."*
> The Jesus Prayer

VOCATIONS SUNDAY *(May)*

Father, you taught us to pray for labourers for the harvest. Grant to your church many committed men and women who will dedicate themselves and their talents, their zeal and their love to the work of the gospel, the service of others and the glory of your name.

MEDIA AND COMMUNICATIONS SUNDAY
(May/June)

You, Lord, chose the written word to speak an eternal gospel to every age. Today is the day of prayer for the media. Give to those who handle words as writers, journalists and broadcasters, integrity and responsibility. May they raise, not lower, our moral standards, may they always stand up for truth.

PENTECOST
(June)

On this special day we offer you our sincere and heartfelt thanks, Lord, for sending down your Holy Spirit to restore and renew mankind. As the power of the Holy Spirit strengthened the faith of your disciples on that first Whit Sunday may it strengthen particularly those people who are struggling with their faith that they may once again come to know the value of the love of Christ. We pray that the Holy Spirit may continue to guide us in caring for those less fortunate than ourselves, bring courage and hope to all those who work for the promotion of Christianity throughout the world and remove ill will and unwillingness to forgive from our hearts.

TRINITY SUNDAY *(June)*

On Trinity Sunday we think of the mystery of the Trinity and the unity of the three persons of God. How, then, can the church be so disunited? We follow one Lord, we hold a common faith, we must long for all denominations to bury their differences and become one.

FATHERS' DAY *(June)*

This is the day on which we remember fathers, Lord. We ask your blessings on all fathers that they will realise their responsibilities, that they will give their children that most precious of all gifts, their time, and that they will always be worthy of the love their children have for them.

We give thanks for our own fathers, for the love and support, the wisdom and guidance we have received from them - and we pray for those who are unable to give thanks; for those who never knew their father and for those who, for whatever reason, feel that their father has hurt them or failed them. May they know your healing presence and the love that will never let us go.

SEA SUNDAY *(July)*

Father, we pray for all sailors, merchant and military. As they experience the extremes of weather, and long periods away from home, may they know your safe keeping, Lord. In times of danger and stress, may they be aware of your presence and know that they can turn to you for strength.

DAY FOR LIFE *(July)*

Lord, we acknowledge the respect due to every human life from conception to death. We pray particularly today for the unborn, the seriously ill and for the very elderly that they will always be respected by those who make our laws. We pray that the right to life from contraception to death will be respected in our society and reflected in our laws and practices. May we cherish, respect and support those in the evening of life.

RACIAL JUSTICE SUNDAY *(September)*

Lord, grant us a breadth of vision and a heart of love. Make our country and our world a place of tolerance and peace. Show us how to rejoice in the variety and richness of your creation and help us to see your reflection in all people, realizing that they and we are your beloved children.

HOME MISSION SUNDAY *(September)*

Lord, give us the will and the courage to publicly share and celebrate our Christian life and faith with those with whom we work and socialise. Let us never be embarrassed to declare our belief in you as our Lord and Saviour.

"I am the vine and you are the branches.
Remain in me, and I in you,
and you will bear much fruit"
John 15:5

HARVEST SUNDAY *(September)*

We give you thanks, Lord, for the fruits of the earth. Make us realise that the resources of the planet are for the benefit of all your children, not just the few. Help us to find better ways of sharing the world's food. We pray for all people of Great Britain who work in agriculture, and also for those who prepare the food for our tables. We pray for those in the countries of the developing world who work on the land, often in backbreaking conditions and for scant reward.

ANIMAL SUNDAY *(October)*

A chance for us to be a voice for the voiceless. Animals cannot speak for themselves; they have to suffer in silence. They suffer through human greed, carelessness and pollution. We alter the balance of nature and diminish the diversity which the Lord created.

We give you thanks, Lord, for all animals and especially for pets who bring so much joy into the lives of young and old alike.

> *"Every creature in the world*
> *will raise our hearts to God*
> *if we look upon it with a good eye"*

St Felix of Cantalice

WORLD MISSION SUNDAY *(October)*

Lord, we pray for religious and medical missionaries who seek to bring all peoples to the knowledge of your love. We pray for vocations to the missionary orders. Your harvest needs labourers, Lord, and we ask that those of us able to give support to their work remember the early slogan of the missions 'A penny can save a life'.

BIBLE SUNDAY *(October/November/December)*

Today is Bible Sunday. We give thanks for this mighty book which is the bedrock of the Christian and the Jewish religions. We remember the prophets, the psalmists, the evangelists who wrote down the word, the translators who made the word widely available and the missionaries who took the word to the far corners of the earth.

Enable us, your children, to grow in knowledge of the Scriptures. Open our hearts to their true meaning and to live the truth fully in our lives. Grant that your word will never be a cause of division among your people but always a source of reconciliation.

PRISONERS' SUNDAY *(November)*

Today is Prisoners Sunday. Jesus tells us that when we serve the prisoner, we serve Christ himself.

Lord, you offer freedom to all people. We pray for all who are captives in prison and for those affected by or involved in their imprisonment. Break the bonds of fear and isolation. Support with your love all prisoners, their families and friends, prison staff and all who care. Heal those who have been wounded by others, especially the victims of crime. Help us to forgive one another, to act justly, to love mercy and to walk humbly together in your strength and spirit.

REMEMBRANCE SUNDAY *(November)*

We pray, Lord, that the young men serving in our armed forces today, though trained and ready to do so, will never have to experience the horrors of war. We also pray that Generals, Admirals and Air Marshals may be ever mindful that they are first and foremost 'keepers of the peace'.

We ask you to guide all Heads of State, those people who rule our countries and our destinies, that they will do so with wisdom and a deep sense of justice.

We pray for the survivors of war, the many servicemen and servicewomen who returned, scarred in mind and body, and for those whose task it is to care for them.

We pray for widows, mothers, fathers and all for whom today will recall a great personal sorrow. Be with them, Lord, and bring them comfort.

We ask you, Lord, never to let us forget all those who fell in the two world wars and in all areas of conflict since.

FEAST OF CHRIST THE KING   *(November)*

Today is the celebration of Christ the King who reigns with you, Father, in heaven. May Christ be our king here on earth and may he be crowned with many crowns by all your people. On this the feast of Christ the King we offer praise and homage to your divine Son who sacrificed his life on the altar of the cross and redeemed the human race. Help us to live by his gospel, and bring us to the joy of his kingdom where he lives for ever and ever.

REJOICE SUNDAY   *(December)*

On this Rejoice Sunday, fill our hearts with joy, Lord, as we prepare to celebrate the birth of the Christ Child. We pray for our family and friends, we thank you for all who care for us and who give us their love. Grant lasting joy to those who give friendship and help in your name.

THE DAY OF PRAYER
FOR EXPECTANT MOTHERS   *(December)*

We pray for all those who carry new life within them. We think especially of those who are having to travel at this time as Mary, the mother of your blessed son, did. May each child, a precious gift, bring joy.

FINAL THOUGHT

Many people who plan to meet God
at the 11th hour
die at half past ten.
Make sure that's not you
and in the meantime
May the Lord walk with you
and keep you safe.